NO

VISIBLE

SCARS

RJ THESMAN

No Visible Scars

Copyright © 2018 RJ Thesman

Cover designed by Sarah Meiers, moshdesigns

All rights reserved.

ISBN-13: 978-1987553505
ISBN-10: 1987553500

Although the germ idea for this book comes from a Bible story, "No Visible Scars" is a contemporary work of fiction. All characters, organizations, places and events in this novel are products of the author's imagination.

All rights reserved. No part of this publication may be reproduced, stored in a retrieval system, or transmitted in any form or by any means – electronic, mechanical, photocopy, recording, or any other – except for brief quotations in printed reviews, without the prior permission of the author.

Printed in the United States of America

No Visible Scars

"*I am fortunate to have been given the opportunity to read 'No Visible Scars' authored by RJ Thesman. The story is compelling. I wanted to read about Abigail, to understand her struggle with domestic abuse. I was saddened by the spiritual abuse from her church that she suffered. I needed to learn the symptoms of abuse and what can be done by a caring community of women.*

This is an eye opener. As I read about Abigail and learned of her struggle I wanted her to find emotional, physical, and spiritual safety. I learned from Abigail's story. I have not been abused, but now I have a story to reference and facts to share. This is a very important book."
– Virginia Ratzlaff, J.D.

"*'No Visible Scars' is a sobering story of a woman stuck in an abusive relationship. RJ Thesman tackles a difficult reality in our society and churches today as she shares this masterpiece. 'No Visible Scars' is for brave souls who want to take an honest look at what abuse looks and feels like. Behind every face is a story begging to be heard. Thesman will help you learn the importance of paying attention. Someone's heart and soul, or maybe even a life, may depend on it.*"
– Amy Beth Salge, CACLC, RN, BSN

"*This is a great read that keeps you thinking positively and gives insight on the sly. While re-reading the Old Testament account of Abigail, Nabal and David, RJ Thesman diagnosed Nabal as the classic abusive husband. 'No Visible Scars' brings this biblical story to today's Kansas City. Thesman has fleshed out the characters to resemble many of our friends with difficult marriages. The intricate character development for Abigail and Nathan helped me understand how abusive marriages can develop* and teaches ideas on how to help empower someone who is being abused. I was engaged in the story and appreciated how I didn't just learn about our seemingly perfect Abigail with the perfect life. This is the only book I've read that even got in to the mind of the husband. For such a painful situation, I felt positive and uplifted while reading."

– Michelle Mirakian, Volunteer Library, GateWay of Hope

"A clever modern day weaving of a tale of man's tyrannical interpretation of scripture and view of submission. RJ Thesman writes, 'The peace of your soul is dependent on becoming the woman God created you to be.' Statistics have shown 1 in 3 women will suffer emotional, verbal or physical abuse in their lifetime. Strength begins when the silence is broken. 'No Visible Scars' will prove to be a valuable resource teaching women the importance of standing up to these forms of abuse and setting boundaries."

– Deborah Forte, Writer

No Visible Scars

Dedicated to the women who embraced their courage and stepped into a new life.

No Visible Scars

No Visible Scars

CHAPTER ONE

Abigail walked past the police station for the third time. She willed herself to draw closer, to yank open the door and state her business. But every cell in her body felt paralyzed. Her heart continued its thumping, louder and more insistent, squeezed by fear.

She had driven all the way to north Kansas City, to a station far from home, to find a police officer who would not know her famous husband. Famous? Yeah, right. More like infamous.

On her fourth trip around the block, she shook her head and clenched her fists. Finally, she pushed through her fear and stormed into the station. Breathless, she stopped in front of the main desk to face a female officer. A woman. She would understand.

"Ma'am, may I help you?"

A shiny badge with Officer Tamara in bold letters. Tamara. A safe person. Was she experienced in domestic problems, this petite woman with caramel-colored hair pulled back into a chignon? No earrings. No makeup. No nonsense.

Abigail swallowed hard. "Uhm, yes, please. I have a question. Uhm…I have a friend who is…concerned about her marriage. Uhm...he's kind of mean, but he doesn't hit her. It's mostly...well...words and emotional stuff and...my friend doesn't know if...is it rape when he's your husband? And if my friend calls 9-1-1, would you come to help her for just words and ...well...what do you think?"

Officer Tamara frowned, then took a sip from her Diet Pepsi, a shiny gold wedding band on her left hand.

A married police officer. That must be safe. She could always threaten him with her gun. Or if there was a problem, the other officers would hurry to defend her. Lucky, lucky Tamara.

The officer stood. She was shorter than Abigail but exuded strength and authority. Abigail stepped back, her stiletto heels a nervous click on the building's tile floor.

"Ma'am, your friend would need to contact us personally and be willing to press charges. Especially regarding domestic abuse, it *is* more difficult when there are no bruises or any visible evidence. It's a he said, she said deal."

Abigail wanted to scream. Maybe she could commit a crime, nothing terrible. Just enough to get her locked up. Far, far away from Nate.

She twirled a section of her hair tight, then tighter until it hurt. The platinum mess Nate loved, so different from her natural shade. She couldn't even own her hair color.

Officer Tamara spoke again. "Here's my card. We *are* trained to handle all sorts of domestic disputes. If your...friend gets in trouble again, have her call me directly. I'll see what we can do."

A mumbled thank you, a grasping of the card. Then Abigail turned and pushed through the door. Gulping air, she wished she could have told Officer Tamara the ugly truth.

※※※

She needed comfort food. The calories wouldn't hurt. In fact, her last medical checkup included a warning from the doctor, "You're getting a bit too thin. Eat some mashed potatoes."

Who wanted potatoes when chocolate sounded better? A quick stop at Sprout's. Only the best ingredients for her mother's brownie recipe.

Back home, she kicked off her Ferragamo heels, set the groceries on the granite countertop, creamed the butter and sugar, folded in the dry ingredients, then the secret ingredient Mama always added.

The rich aroma of chocolate floated through the kitchen, a reminder of the past when life was safe. A warm-from-the-oven brownie. A glass of milk. Laughter. The smell and taste of her mother's love.

She bit into another brownie. Three, but who was counting? "He was perfect, Mama…at the beginning. Such a sensitive and gentle lover, the man I wanted to grow old with, the guy who met all my needs. I felt secure, loved, taken care of. I wanted to finish my degree and become a teacher, but Nate talked me into marrying him. He cares about the elderly, but not about me. What shall I do? Give him another chance? Try to talk to him again?"

No Visible Scars

A few hours later, Abigail forced herself to finish dinner. She swallowed the last of her chicken salad, washed the pan and arranged the supper dishes in the dishwasher. Nate had gulped his food, then mumbled something about the quarterly spreadsheets as he left the dining room. She took another swallow of Merlot and clenched her fists, her nails biting into her palms. Time for a heart-to-heart with her husband.

His mobile office already spread out on the sofa. He leafed through some papers from the office, occasionally grunted and marked something with his pen. His pointer finger tapped on his thigh, long legs sprawled under the glass coffee table.

Abigail sat on the edge of her rocker recliner and watched him work. She clutched the taupe fuzzy pillow to her chest. Tried to knead away her nerves. Nate could have been a basketball player, long and lean, in great shape. His wavy brown hair always perfect except for one strand that fell forward like an apostrophe. He shuffled more papers and crossed out a line item. Poked at his iPad.

Abigail noted his frustration. Something must be slightly wrong. He was always focused on business, on the brilliant idea he and his best friend, David, invented their senior year of college. The Villas de Comfort: a national franchise of assisted living facilities, meeting the needs of aging baby boomers. He seemed to genuinely care for the elderly. Not so much for his wife.

No Visible Scars

She leaned forward, still clutching the pillow. "Are we heading in the right direction, Nate?"

"What do you mean? Everything seems fine to me." He circled a number, then flipped a page of the spreadsheet.

"We once talked about making a difference in the world."

He dropped the paper and frowned."We *are* making a difference. I give a donation to the church every Sunday and we help lots of families at the Villas. What are you talking about?" He flipped another page.

"Oh, I don't know. I feel like something is missing, and I can't seem to find my way back to it. Maybe more of a connection to people, to help them in more practical ways, to teach their children and share kindness with the world. Especially with the children."

"Humph. Sounds like social worker stuff. That's not what we're about, Abby. We'll use our influence to make lots of money."

His usual response. Didn't they live in a beautiful house in Leawood, the cream of Johnson County's crop of million dollar homes? Didn't she appreciate how hard he worked so they could each drive a new car?

She pulled back and settled in the recliner. "Is that really what it's all about? The money?"

"Of course it is. Money gives us the power to make choices, to have options. Then we give it to the needy. Making money is the most practical way to make a difference."

"I agree that we need money. I never want to be poor again. It was hard growing up with a single mom, never knowing my father, living in a dinky apartment and saving every penny. But doesn't influence involve more than cash? Feeling good about ourselves has to involve more than our bank account."

"Don't be insipid, Abby. Ask anybody in a nonprofit or a church. It's money that makes things happen. Now leave me alone. I'm busy."

She wanted to think more about his statements, talk about her own vision, the desires of her heart. But she couldn't push too hard. She knew better. She slapped the recliner down, padded into the kitchen and listened to the dishes rattle as they washed.

Nate was always so intent on his personal capital, and he was brilliant at business development. Who was she to judge? She enjoyed the money, too. Nate's success affected her future. With their growing bank account, she could someday return to school and finish her education degree without the burden of school loans. Maybe even acceptance to grad school. Mama would be so proud.

He called her insipid. She didn't deserve that adjective just because she disagreed with him.

His voice from the living room. "Bring me a Perrier, would ya'?"

She reached into the fridge and pulled out a bottle, then another one for herself. As she handed Nate his drink, he stroked her arm. She wasn't in the mood. She settled back into her recliner and opened the latest Rainbow Rowell novel. If she escaped into the words of a good story, she could forget that "insipid" comment.

Maybe she was being too sensitive. He was always mentioning how she overreacted to his comments, how she corrected his mistakes on paperwork at the office, how she needed a little more blonde in her hair. In fact, she couldn't remember when he last gave her a compliment. But then, she couldn't remember the last kind word she had spoken to him either.

Maybe if she tried harder, respected her husband and his leadership qualities, she might feel better. More in sync with Nate and his goals. Yet her goals were important, too. She sighed loudly, hoping he might notice.

Nothing. He punched more numbers into the iPad and sifted through more papers.

It was impossible to balance everything at the office with everything she wanted for herself. Nate wanted her to continue as the executive assistant at the Villas. All those years ago, she had let him talk her out of finishing her degree. Now he controlled everything, and when he drank too much, when his stress and anger spilled out…. It wasn't pretty.

Maybe he would listen to her if she mentioned she had driven to the police station, talked with an officer. She turned back to the first page of the novel. Start over. What was happening in this story?

Nate finished his Perrier then topped it off with a martini. Then another. He would soon begin slurring his words and stumble upstairs to the bedroom.

In spite of the gnarly feeling that something was wrong with her dreams of happily-ever-after, Abigail clung to her marriage. Surely Nate would someday change back to

No Visible Scars

the man she had fallen in love with, the man who cared about her opinions and spent time listening to her. She would not, could not repeat the direction of the past and fall into the shadow of her mother's poverty. She would do whatever it took to keep her marriage secure, even if she lost herself in the process.

Insipid. Really? She crossed her legs and frowned. Back to the first page.

※※※

12:03. Just past midnight. Abigail slipped out of bed and waited a moment before grabbing her satin robe. No interruption of Nate's snores, so she hurried down the steps and turned on the lights to the living room.

She opened her wooden crafting case and chose a burgundy gel pen. Still no sound from upstairs. Her words scrolled across the parchment page. *Happy Anniversary to my beloved Husband.*

Beloved. Hmm. She crumpled the page and started another one. *Happy Anniversary to my Husband.*

Something had changed in her marriage, and she couldn't figure it out. Didn't know how to correct what she did not understand. Everything about Nate seemed so intense. She never knew which husband would come home: the stressed-out-from-work guy, the spiritual leader straight from a deacon's meeting or the hidden anger guy who gave her the silent treatment.

Insipid? As if her opinions, her words didn't matter. As if the marriage was a teeter totter in the park and she was the one always getting bumped off at the bottom.

Crumple up another paper. Keep it simple. *Happy Anniversary.*

She closed the card inside the case, then hid it under the sofa cushion. The fuzzy taupe pillow patted in place, his Forbes magazine on the leather ottoman.

Everything as Nate wanted it. Always.

No Visible Scars

CHAPTER TWO

Abigail could not figure it out. One minute they were talking about anniversary plans, and the next.... She looked at herself in the mirror and whispered, "I don't understand what I'm doing wrong."

It happened so fast. Nate's red face, the way he jerked his shirt off the hanger and yelled, "Can't you do anything right? I've told you a hundred times my white shirts go next to the Oxford blue. You're so stupid!" He threw the hanger at her feet.

She bent down to pick it up. "For Pete's sake, one shirt out of order. Maybe you're the one who put it in the wrong place."

He grabbed her hair. She flinched, and he yanked. Hard. Quick tears at the sudden pain. "Stop it!"

He flicked strands of her hair in the trash. "It's your fault. Hurry up and get ready. We have a reservation." He stomped down the stairs. The door to the garage slammed.

Now he waited in the car, every few minutes mashing on the horn. Let him wait a little longer. She stared at the bald spot reflected in the mirror. Her hand shook as she dabbed at the last of the blood that oozed from her scalp. It could have been worse.

She parted her hair on the other side and pulled it over to cover the empty place, fastened it with a barrette. That seemed to work. For now.

No one would suspect her husband had just graduated from calling her names to pulling out her hair.

She finished dressing, blew her nose and wiped away the last of her tears. The car horn again. She hurried down the stairs.

They drove to the Country Club Plaza in silence. She had no desire to celebrate their ninth anniversary at the Melting Pot, but Nate was hungry for fondue. He ordered for both of them, "The fondue feast for two, the salmon entree and a bottle of Merlot."

Her appetite disappeared like chalk lines rubbed out on a sidewalk.

As the waitress brought the various breads, fruits, vegetables and cheeses, Abigail watched a young couple in the corner. A plateful of strawberries sat between them. They took turns dipping fruit into the chocolate and feeding each other. Obviously just engaged. The diamond on the girl's left hand sparkled in the light from the overhead LED lamps.

Nine years. How odd that the years moved along so quickly when every day seemed a thousand hours long. By the end of nine years, she had hoped for a happy family, for a couple of children, for the completion of her degree and a good job in a school. Now, all that time was gone. And bits of herself had disappeared piece by piece, one hopeless day at a time.

She forced herself to eat. Although the salmon filet tasted delicious, her stomach felt sour. The scowl plastered

No Visible Scars

on Nate's face announced his displeasure with her. He said little, until she dropped a grape into the cheese sauce. "Do you have to be so clumsy? Can't you do anything right?"

She fished it out and wrapped it in her napkin. Delicious food wasted. Not so delicious company. What was there to talk about after nine years?

At one time, Nate acted as attentively as the young man in the corner. He gently touched his fiancée's hair. That sweet young girl could never imagine her husband-to-be might someday pull out a patch of her shiny curls.

One minute you cut into the wedding cake, the next minute he calls you, "Insipid." The cycle spirals through the years like a tornado that can't make up its mind, up then down, benign then disastrous. And afterward, always, Nate apologizes. As if a simple "I'm sorry" can make up for years of put downs.

Just as he did now. "All right, I'm sorry. I didn't mean to grab your head like that. I guess your hair got caught in my watch. If you'd wear your hair up, it wouldn't hang down and get in my way."

Abigail felt for her barrette. A slight throb of pain underneath. "I already color it the way you like. Do I have to wear it in a certain style?"

"I'm just sayin'. With it hanging down like that, it's easy for my Rolex to get caught in it."

It was always her fault. She ate too much. She didn't eat enough. She could put on a few pounds. She needed to be careful not to grow a muffin top. Wasn't she grateful for all he provided?

No Visible Scars

She smoothed her napkin over her black silk pants, then peered at the young couple smooching in the corner. The girl wore a tulip yellow top that accented her brown hair. Red highlights peeked through the strands.

If only she could wear something that bright. She always wore Nate's version of professional dress code. Black blazers and taupe or beige tops, black slacks and the appropriate pumps. "Look the part of an executive assistant," he said.

In the spring, when the Kansas landscape reversed its drab browns into the lush of green farmland and pink redbud blooms, Nate relented a bit. He let her wear the creamier versions of taupe jackets, a single strand of pearls hanging over the same beige tops and black slacks. Top of the line clothes, the best he let her buy.

Each day after work, she quickly changed into her favorite workout pants and a T-shirt. She walked barefoot on their herringbone floors with a toe ring on her second digit, right foot. Something about that toe ring gave her an identity, helped her remember underneath the beige and black office coverings lay a somewhat funky personality.

She wriggled her toes underneath the table now, feeling for the toe ring, trying to remind herself of who she used to be, the unique identity at the core of her being. Before Nate. Before nine years of living as his version of the obedient and submissive wife.

How she longed to leave the corporate world and escape to a smaller place, where tiny people learned alphabet letters and experimented with colors. Where happiness resounded in the laughter of recess, the hugs of chubby arms at the end of the day.

But Nate was supposed to be her first priority and her marriage ordained by God. That's what everybody at church said. All their marriage needed was a commitment to trust God, read the Bible and stay connected to other Christians. They were just going through a rough patch. Every married couple experienced tough times.

Nate reached across the table with a tiny silver box in his hand. "Happy anniversary, Abby. Be sure to wear this to the Villas Christmas party. I want everyone to notice my beautiful wife and how I buy her the best."

She lifted the lid. Shining in its setting was an open heart necklace, one of the styles advertised on television. Silver. Nate's color. Not hers. She preferred gold, but perhaps she had never told him. How could a man know her heart if she couldn't be honest with him?

"It's lovely. Thank you."

"Put it on. Now."

She reached behind her neck and found the clasp. She fumbled inside her purse and pulled out a card and a long, rectangular box. "I made the card," she said.

"Hmm," Nate said, seemingly unimpressed with the effort she put into the tiny stencils of hearts and ivy. He opened the box. "A pen? You bought me a pen?"

"It's crafted from wood scraps found at the base of the Grand Canyon. I thought you might like something truly unique."

"Oh, okay." He signaled for the waiter. "We're ready for our check."

The young couple stared into each other's eyes with no need for conversation, no forced sentences, no expected thank you's. Their meal completed, they seemed in no hurry to leave but took the time to revel in each other, to enjoy the moment.

Abigail sighed and followed Nate to the car.

Before bed, she dabbed a bit more hydrogen peroxide on the wound, then looked at the Kleenex. No more blood, but still a sting. Hopefully, it would heal before the party in two days. The annual Christmas celebration for the staff of Villas de Comfort, Nate's responsibility and his biggest night of the year. The one time he allowed her to dress in something sparkly, but still in the appropriate black or sometimes a satiny taupe.

She would dress up for him again. Play the part of trophy wife.

CHAPTER THREE

She checked her list for the Christmas party but didn't really need it. She knew how the evening would play out. Their spacious home already shone with the newest and brightest of holiday décor.

Remind the maid to polish all the furniture and supply each of the five bathrooms with extra toilet paper. Make sure all the caterers arrived on time. Arrange the hors d'oeuvres on silver platters throughout the living/dining area. The vintage wines and Perrier waited on the floor of the walk-in pantry. Impress the guests. Make Nate happy.

Of course, her brownies would take center stage. One Christmas four years ago, she decided to resurrect her mother's recipe and served brownies as a surprise dessert. Now they were the headliners of the party's traditional fare.

No one but Abigail knew the secret ingredient, not even Nate. She memorized the recipe because she wanted one thing he could never take from her. It represented the special bond she had shared with her mother: memories of a warm kitchen, the giggles that erupted as they cracked eggs and melted butter, the final indulgence with organic cocoa and dark chocolate chunks blended into a square of rich

No Visible Scars

flavor. And the secret ingredient that kept them moist, long after other brownies turned into dark bricks.

"These are heavenly," the guests always exclaimed. "Tell us how you make them. What is your secret?"

Abigail would merely wag her pointer finger at them and try to ignore the crooked direction of said finger, the cock-eyed digit Nate grabbed one night and broke.

"An accident," he said, as they sat in the emergency room, waiting for the young resident who obviously had never set a bone.

"A terrible accident," agreed Abigail, fairly certain if she hadn't asked Nate once again about going back to school, her finger might still appear straight. It was all her fault, he said,
that crooked pointer finger he called "a cute little quirk" in public, her "ugly finger" in private.

She would still be making brownies with her mother and stirring the batter with a straight finger if that drunk driver hadn't crossed the median in the Grandview Triangle and smashed into her mother's VW bug.

Even now, working on her party list, Abigail marveled how she made it through that week, the visitation and memorial service. The people from church were terrific with their food, cards and sympathetic hugs. Nate acted like a devoted husband. He thanked people for coming and arranged leftover casseroles in Tupperware coffins. Leftovers she would never eat. Dead enzymes in plastic. Everything dead. Just like her mother.

Only the brownies brought solace. She made huge batches, trying to remember her mother's voice and copy the

No Visible Scars

way she spread the batter on the aluminum pans. She took her "grieving" brownies to meetings at church and shared them with the staff at work.

Then Nate grew tired of it. "For cryin' out loud, Abby. The whole frickin' house smells like chocolate. Stop making brownies."

So she complied. Her mother had lain in the ground, covered by dead flowers for several months. Abigail shed tears until she finally dried up inside and out, as raw as the February day when Mama last breathed.

She would make her brownies again for the Villas party, decorate the platter with some greenery and place a few raspberries on the side to please Nate. He loved raspberries. Otherwise, after the guests left, if everything didn't go as planned, if any glitch happened in the evening that kept Nate from his place of honor in his own home—Abigail knew she would pay for it. How many more fingers could he break until someone noticed?

She scribbled a note to remind the caterers to bring plenty of raspberries. Might as well cover all her bases.

∂❥∂❥∂❥

"Make sure everything is ready," Nate ordered. "I'm gonna' take my shower. "

Abigail hurried through each room of the house, her eye for detail catching a stray ornament that had fallen to the floor, a gilded feather that floated from its perch to the coffee table.

Each room featured a different Christmas tree, decorated with a particular theme. Even in the bathrooms, tiny trees sat near the guest towels, expertly accessorized with the colors of the accent tiles.

The living room tree with its shiny purple balls, an occasional peacock feather to give it that whimsical yet luxurious flair. She checked the twinkle lights hung in bright scallops from the tray ceiling. Every bulb perfect, shining warmth against the cold sterility of the white walls.

In the dining room, a tree covered with gold ornaments reflected colored spectrums from the crystal chandelier. Abigail spaced all fifteen chairs exactly thirty-two inches apart from the center of each place setting. Nate's etiquette. "Guests have to feel like they have their own space."

She ached to feel the same, to own her own space. Somewhere. Someday.

In the kitchen, a tree festooned with gingerbread men shared its spicy aroma with the cranberry punch on the granite counter. She reached behind the tree and fingered one of the gingerbread men. Turned him upside down. Nate would never see it, but she would know. Rebellion flashed a joyous tingle up her spine.

She had worked for weeks with a designer, making sure this year's trees outdid the ones from the year before. Guests often snapped photos from their smart phones to share on social media and bragged about the luxuries of Nate's house.

"We were there…the annual Christmas gala for the Villas de Comfort…unbelievable trees and the food…amazing!"

No Visible Scars

"Did you notice the tree on the deck? The biggest blue spruce I've ever seen, decorated with peanut butter bagels and wild bird seed for the 'outdoor' guests. Fabulous!"

Abigail finished dressing, then loosely pinned her chignon so a few tendrils escaped down the back and on the sides. She had backcombed the area around the once bald spot while her side part covered the flaw. Then a small hairpiece, clipped into place, made the blonde mass look even thicker and full of body.

If Nate noticed, he said nothing except for the usual command on her clothing choices. "This year, I want you to look especially nice. Wear the black satin dress with the necklace I gave you for our anniversary."

She slipped into the dress and frowned at herself in the free-standing mirror. The dress gave her a stylish flair but the necklace felt like a chain, a shackle to Nate and his pretend life. If only she could wear shiny gold, anything but his favorite black.

"Hurry up," Nate commanded as he finished with his tie. "Guests will be coming soon."

They stood together in the front foyer, his arm around her waist. The happy couple in their lovely home. He smiled as each of the staff arrived. Then a loud "Merry Christmas" as members of the board of directors stepped across the threshold.

She kissed the cheeks of women, smelled their various perfumes. "Such a lovely dress," she said. "A beautiful color on you and so festive."

No Visible Scars

Small talk she didn't care about. "Isn't it a beautiful evening? Can you believe it's Christmas already?"

The door opened again and Abigail shivered as cold air rushed in. One of the newer employees stepped forward and gripped Nate's hand. "Welcome to our home," Nate said. "Have you met my lovely wife, Abby?"

She gritted her teeth, yet beamed her trophy wife smile. Her role as another of Nate's possessions, an accessory to his beautiful home.

How she hated it when he called her Abby, but he always chose nicknames when addressing people. His own moniker was the prime example. "Call me Nate," he had told her when they first met. "Nathan sounds old-fashioned and stilted. I'm on the move, heading for success. Nothing old-fashioned about me."

Abigail loved her given name, with its lilt of three syllables that reminded her of her mother. "I gave you a strong name," Mama said, "because that's my hope for you. Strength and courage."

What would Mama think if she saw her now? No courage evident. No apparent strength.

Abigail numbed down the disappointment in herself and pasted on her party smile. She moved toward the dining room. "So nice of you to join us," she said, nodding to each guest. "Please make yourself at home."

Nate followed Samuel and his wife, Roberta, into the dining room to make sure they were seated comfortably with plenty of hors d'oeuvres arranged on their plates. Samuel, president of the board of directors, winked at Abigail as she handed him one of her brownies. "My dear, you have teased us once again with your wonderful treats. I look forward to these every year."

"Yes indeed," said Roberta. "Samuel is always asking our chef to reproduce them, but somehow the end product isn't as tasty as yours. I don't know how many recipes we've tried."

"I'm so glad you like them. The recipe came from my mother, so they're special to me."

Roberta patted Abigail's hand. "What a wonderful legacy!"

Nate greeted more guests and Abigail strolled through the living room. When would David arrive? Usually late to any event, this year's Christmas party was no exception. As Marketing Director for the company, David knew how to meet and greet. He seemed to put everyone at ease, especially his collection of lovelies. No one could guess which girl David would bring each year.

One of the ornaments fell off the living room tree, so Abigail bent to pick it up. She hung it on a secure branch, then flinched as Nate grabbed her elbow. "We need more brownies," he said, as he steered her away from the tree. He smiled at one of the secretaries who passed by and at the same time muttered, "Can't you do anything right? Keep the guests happy, for Pete's sake. Don't let this plate get empty again."

Rushing into the pantry to retrieve more of her treats, she handed the tin to one of the caterers. "Please keep the plates filled," she said. "Mr. Calebian wants plenty of everything for the guests."

Just as she rejoined the group chatting in the living room, David entered with his date. He carried his guitar, another part of their Christmas tradition. Every year, he sang "Silent Night" with the traditional guitar background, then led everyone in several rousing carols.

"Abigail," he said, as he shrugged out of his coat and handed it to the valet. "This is Michele, who decided to accompany me tonight to this delightful soiree."

"Welcome, Michele. Please make yourself at home." Abigail was dazzled by the beauty of David's date. As always, he picked the loveliest of women. Michele stood a few inches taller than David but that didn't seem to bother her. She gave off an aura of confidence, her black hair shiny and long, draped over the shoulder of her Christmas red gown.

Abigail felt a twinge of regret. Next to Michele, she felt small and envious of her freedom to wear such a bright color.

David's auburn hair caught the light of the hallway. The reddish strands reflected Christmas cheer along with his green tie, brown reindeer dancing up and down its borders. "Abigail is our executive assistant," he said to Michele. "She's amazing. We couldn't operate without her." His eyes shone with genuine gratitude, his voice like a gentle thought.

At the unexpected compliment, Abigail blushed but recovered as Nate walked through the archway. "Well, Dave," he said, "I see you finally made it. Some of our guests were asking for the traditional carols a minute ago. And who is with you tonight?"

"Michele, meet our illustrious VP of Development. This is Nate, the husband of Abigail. We've been buddies since college. It was Nate's idea to start the Villas de Comfort. He saw how the need would increase through the years and how we could help more of the elderly folks. He's the driving force behind the company, except for your father, of course."

"Father?" asked Nate as he shook Michele's hand.

"Yep," explained David. "Saul, our beneficent CEO, is Michele's father. He let me borrow her for the evening." David's hazel eyes danced with excitement.

"I wouldn't call it borrowing," stated Michele, her voice a confident airing of beauty and sophistication. "More like a loan, out on approval."

"In that case," said David. "I approve wholeheartedly." They laughed together as they joined hands and strolled into the dining room. "You have to taste these brownies, babe," he said as he grabbed one off a plate. "Abigail makes them. They're amazing."

Nate hovered near Abigail's shoulder. "Another girlfriend. You'd think by this time, Dave would have settled down. It would look better for the company and maybe help our bottom line. We're supposed to be a family business." He peered sideways. "Have you checked your hair lately? It looks a bit, I don't know, askew on the top. Go take care of it. We'll be singing carols soon and giving out the Christmas bonuses."

Abigail moved surreptitiously to the half bath near the laundry room. Some of her carefully arranged hair tufts seemed a bit out of place. She wet her fingers and pressed the hair into place, readjusted the hairpiece, then quickly joined Nate in the living room. She knew her place for the traditional carol-singing and handing out of bonus checks. Standing beside her husband. The dutiful wife fulfilling her role.

David sat at the front of the living room and swallowed another bite of brownie. He tipped his head toward Abigail as if to thank her for the treat, then reached for his wine glass and gulped a couple of swallows. Nothing too staid about David.

He strummed his guitar, a quiet chording similar to the original version of "Silent Night."Abigail hummed along but enjoyed listening to the guests sing all four verses. Then "Joy to the World" and "Jingle Bells" with David's strong voice leading them.

After the last chorus of "Oh what fun it is to ride in a one horse open sleigh," Abigail sighed. She wished the music could continue into the night.

Nate moved toward the mantel and reached behind the cloisonné Santa Claus to retrieve a bundle of envelopes. As he read the names Abigail had printed in calligraphy, those particular staff members came forward. Nate smiled and seemed to enjoy giving bonuses to his most dedicated workers. Everyone clapped when the last one was handed out.

Abigail, of course, received no envelope, no bonus, no congratulations from her husband for another year of service. A bonus for her would have been ludicrous anyway since Nate controlled all the finances. She was lucky he gave her some pocket money once a month. Every other purchase went straight to his credit card.

She was grateful for the security he provided, a roof over her head and all her needs met. At least, the needs that could be bought.

But it was her inner soul that felt needy, so painful each breath hurt. Hope lived so far away, she couldn't imagine reaching for it. Her identity seemed yanked from within, like the stubbly hair hiding underneath her hairpiece.

Nate stood by the mantel, drank his wine and shook hands, wallowing in the gratitude of his employees. Abigail recognized the irony. She was grateful Nate possessed the power and resources to award his employees. Yet inwardly, his soul-sucking attitude underscored her emptiness. She could not imagine herself confident and free like Michele, who conversed with Samuel and Roberta, her flashy red gown an accent to the white sofa.

The guests began to leave, so Abigail joined Nate at the door. Her shoulders tensed, but she tried to relax as they thanked everyone for coming and recited the usual pleasantries.

"Yes, of course. Let's do lunch some time."

"Thank you so much. We loved having you. Come back again."

Samuel helped Roberta into her coat. "I'm still waiting for that recipe," he said as he winked.

Abigail giggled. "You know I'm not going to give you the secret to my brownies." She kissed the old venerate on the cheek, then did the same with Roberta. Such dear people.

David grabbed his guitar and pocketed another brownie. He took Michele's hand. "Thanks for another great Christmas party, Nate. You and Abigail always do it spot on. Let's visit an art gallery sometime or go to a concert, the four of us."

"Like we have that kind of time," said Nate.

Michele gave Abigail the obligatory kiss on the cheek. "Lovely home," she said.

"So nice to meet you."

"See you at the office," called Nate as David and Michele strolled toward his Jeep Wrangler. Michele waved at Abigail, who waved back, wishing she could leave with them.

Now that the guests were gone, she knew the drill. Nate would complain about the one Christmas cookie, the bell with sugary beads that fell off the counter or the shrimp roll-ups that didn't stay rolled or the way one of the guests talked incessantly or whatever else upset him about the evening.

But this time, he surprised her. "Nice party, huh?" he asked as the caterers gathered up the last of the food remnants and emptied plates into trash cans.

"Yes, of course. Everyone always loves your Christmas party."

He seemed satisfied and carried a wine bottle up the spiral steps toward their bedroom. She knew what came next. He would finish the bottle and maybe another one, then roll over on top of her and demand that she make him feel good, thank him for the sex and promise to love him always. It was their routine. Another piece of Abigail's soul-killing and mind-numbing life.

But she would put it off as long as possible. She thanked the last of the caterers, then handed them the tips Nate had stuffed into their envelopes. "Keep the help happy," he always said. "Then they'll return next year and do a bang-up job."

As she turned off the kitchen lights and checked the digital security codes on the doors, she looked at the reflection of the Christmas tree in the corner. What a beautiful symbol of this time of year when families celebrated together. Tears threatened. She missed her mother so much, it was a physical ache in her chest. Maybe God would bless her with a heart attack and end the pitiful life she lived.

"Merry Christmas, Mama. I wish you were here," she whispered and seemed to hear a voice wishing the same to her.

"Be strong," it said, then disappeared into the dark recesses of the living room.

"Abby," came the slurred voice of her husband. "Get up here."

Yeah. Merry Christmas and here's wishing for a happier New Year.

No Visible Scars

CHAPTER FOUR

On the way to work, Abigail broached the subject. "Now that the Christmas party is over, do you think we could talk about my college degree? I'd really like to get started next semester."

Nate took the corner too fast, then swore as the right front tire bumped over the curb. "I've told you before, you don't have time for that. Besides, teachers don't make decent money. You're needed at the Villas front office, and that's where you'll stay."

"But Nate...."

"I mean it, Abby. Stop talking about going back to school. Discussion ended."

She stared out the window as he sped toward Overland Park and the corporate headquarters. She swallowed disappointment as green and red lights winked from store front displays. A giant Santa waved at her. She refused to wave back.

At the office, she slammed a drawer and caught her fingernail in it. As she filed it down, tiny flakes of nail dust settled on her black slacks. Powerless, the new adjective that described her. Just like the nail dust. She ached for life to head in a different direction, but every time she tried to move forward, she smashed against the brick wall named Nate.

She flipped through Excel charts that recorded every branch of the corporation. Point and click. Point and click. She didn't need to work for the money. Nate's salary and benefits took care of everything. But he wanted her with him, front and center every day.

Point and click. Point and click. She jammed her finger into the mouse, wishing she could write alphabet letters on a white board or gather little people around her for a reading of "The Cat in the Hat."

Point and click. Point and click. How she hated the electronic mouse that consumed her days.

Sure, her job was important, sometimes even enjoyable. Occasionally, a call came in from one of the sites in Iowa or Illinois, last week from the new facility in Michigan. She had chatted with another admin. "You're on security lockdown? Is everyone safe? How can we help you?"

She rifled through company greeting cards and chose one to send to the stressed-out Michigan employees, to remind them the corporate office appreciated how they provided respite to the elderly. Theirs was a noble profession, a good work. But sending cards and fixing charts felt empty, as dry as the emery board she tossed back in her purse.

After several hours of Excel charts, the digital clock on the right bottom of her computer posted eleven fifty-eight. Almost time to meet her best friend, Cassie, for their lunch date. Nate allowed her one lunch hour per month to escape from the office.

Abigail smiled as she remembered how she met Cassie at a networking event. They bumped into each other at the salad bar as they both reached for the ranch dressing. Cassie laughed and said, "We must be of the same mind." From there it was only a few shared condiments and a trip to the ladies' room to cement their friendship.

Cassie and her husband, Rick, lived in a comfortable Overland Park split level. Rick owned a landscaping company, "Sod and Such," so their lawn always looked beautiful with curb appeal boasting a myriad of perennials and colorful annuals.

Noon. She quickly powered off her computer and reached for her Brighton bag. "I'll be back by 1:00," she wrote on a yellow Post-it note at her desk. "Lunch with Cassie."

Nate always checked her desk on his way to lunch, to make sure everything looked tidy. "Efficiency starts at the entry level," he said. "No clutter allowed."

She maneuvered through the lunch hour traffic and deftly parked her Honda Acura in front of the Happy Grounds Café. She and Cassie had discovered the quaint out-of-the-way place in Westport on another lunch excursion and it soon became their favorite place.

The Happy Grounds was their escape from jobs neither of them liked. Currently working as a paralegal, Cassie hoped to someday own an art studio. She loved to play around with clays and pastels, dip her hands in mud and swirl it around a pedestal. But mostly, she wanted to display the art of others, to help beginning artists develop their brands and move toward their dreams.

The difference in Cassie's life was that Rick supported her goals. As soon as they finished paying off their business loan, he promised to help her look for a storefront and set up her business. "Smart Art" she wanted to call it. She was already doodling with a logo for her business cards and brochures.

Abigail locked her car and hurried inside. She always felt a measure of hope when she met with Cassie. She ordered her usual, "Grande iced chai and a tuna fish on rye, please." She found a table in the corner, sipped her chai and settled back into the Bentwood chair. She closed her eyes and savored the spice as it slowly rivered down her throat.

When she opened her eyes, Cassie stood at the register, paying for her lunch. "Sorry I'm late," she said as she plopped into a chair and took the lid off her mocha latte. She swirled her tongue around the inside of the cup until all the foam collected in one spot. Then she gulped several swallows. "Couldn't get away from the office. Then I spent some time in the bathroom, barfing up my breakfast."

"Are you okay? You look so pale and a little…I don't know…green. No insult intended."

Cassie waved her left hand, her simple gold wedding band contrasting with the eclectic mood ring on her middle finger. "It'll pass. Once I eat something again, I'll be right as rain. In fact," she leaned across the table and her eyes twinkled, "I have a secret."

"Tell me. I need to think of something besides work and my boring life."

"Think about it. I'm pale, throwing up my breakfast, a secret...."

"Oh my gosh. You're pregnant."

"Bingo!"

Abigail grabbed Cassie's hand and squeezed. "I'm so happy for you. This is wonderful news." At the same time, the hidden place that held hopes for her own child, ached.

"So are you and Nate planning a family? I'd love it if you and I were pregnant together."

Abigail shook her head. "Not going to happen. Nate doesn't like kids."

Cassie frowned. "What's not to like? Oh, for Pete's sake, I know they're a lot of work and I've heard women complain about losing sleep, stretch marks and the dreaded twenty hours of labor, but really...no kids at all?"

"Nate says kids are too messy. He had a vasectomy so we wouldn't have an 'accident' as he called it."

"Oh, honey," said Cassie, a tear caught on her eyelid. "I'm so sorry. But he can have it reversed. Right?"

Abigail cleared the sorrow out of her throat. "I doubt that will ever happen." It was probably better this way. What if he pulled out their daughter's hair or yelled obscenities at their son? She rocked back and forth, tried to numb down the pain. "I don't want to talk about it. But Cassie, I'm so excited for you. How far along are you?"

"Barely ten weeks. I haven't even gained any weight. Rick thinks that's going to be the fun part, watching me grow fat and hugging my belly every night. In fact, he's already started to do that." She giggled and took a bite of her ham sandwich. A dill pickle plopped out. She grabbed it and dropped it into her mouth. "They tell me pickles will become an obsession," she said, talking with her mouth full.

Abigail bit off a small piece of her tuna sandwich, then took another sip of her chai. "So what happens to Smart Art? Are you still going to plan for your business? Can you do that and be a mom?"

"Of course. I'm not giving up on my dream just because I'm currently with child. In fact, I talked to a woman last week who has a ceramics shop. She sets up a play pen in her office and takes the kid with her to work. Besides, if I don't accomplish my goal, how will I ever teach my child to follow her dreams?"

Abigail nodded. "Good point."

"I have Rick's support and he can watch the baby when I'm busy. We'll work it out together."

"You're lucky to have Rick."

"Don't I know it. Oh, my stars, I almost forgot." Cassie reached into her Vera Bradley bag and pulled out a flyer. She unfolded it and slapped it on the table. "Look at this. I think we should do it."

Abigail picked up the flyer. The graphic of a book cover took up most of the page, then a small blurb and an address. She read it aloud, "Join us for our next Life Limits Class. Learn how to set healthy boundaries. Gain control of your life. At the Hope Gathering, Westport."

"Hope Gathering? What is that?" She handed the flyer back to Cassie.

"I Googled it last night. It's a nonprofit, two neighborhoods away from here. Evidently, they teach this Life Limits Class twice a year. I called the executive director this morning and talked to her. She said women need to have a refresher on setting boundaries because we have such a hard time saying, 'No.' We want to do everything and be everything and eventually, we burn out because we don't know how to set healthy limits in our lives. Listen to me. I sound like an advertisement and we haven't even seen this place yet.

"It's only fifty dollars for eight weeks of training. I'll spot you the dough, because I know Nate probably won't let you have the money. Let's do this. I may need some reminders about boundaries, especially with the baby coming."

Abigail had trusted Cassie with some of the facts about her marriage. Cassie knew Nate controlled the money, and he wouldn't let her go back to school and finish her degree. Cassie also knew she hated to be called Abby almost as much as she hated her job.

But she had never confided the full extent of what she lived with. She didn't share about the fear she felt when Nate came home and guzzled a bottle of wine. She never talked about the bald spot and fortunately, it quickly grew out. She had never told Cassie how late at night, she tried to figure out how to escape from the mess her life had become.

She picked at her sandwich. "Nate would never let me go to a Life Limits Class, especially if they're talking about boundaries."

"Look, my friend, what if he doesn't know exactly where you are on this night? Wouldn't he let you go to a Bible study at my church? You could tell him that's where we are. He'll never know. And I'll bet this Life Limits class includes some Bible verses, so that part is true."

"Lie to him? Should I do that?"

"Why not? I don't tell Rick every single thing I do. Look, this is a good idea. The executive director told me it could change our lives."

Abigail picked up the flyer and scanned it. "Change our lives. I don't know. Sure, it sounds great, and I'd love to do this with you. But...I don't know...."

This class felt like an adventure, a chance to get away from Nate and his stupid rules for a couple of hours. Her heart beat faster. She took a couple of deep breaths. She had never lied to Nate about anything. Yet this felt like her last chance, her one opportunity to march toward her dreams and feel alive again. "Okay. I'll do it." She slapped the flyer on the table and fist-pumped Cassie. "How do we start?"

Cassie finished her pickle and stifled a burp in her napkin. "Let's practice what you'll say to Nate. Then it will seem natural and you won't have to worry about it."

A tiny smidgen of Mama's voice seemed to penetrate the smooth jazz music playing in the background, "Be brave."

Step into that place of courage and give it a try. What was the worst Nate could do? He already yelled at her. "Okay," she said. "Let's practice."

"Great!" Cassie rolled up the last of their lunch mess and tossed it into a trash can. "So, we're going to a Bible study, right? Let's say we'll be learning about, oh I don't know...the book of John. That's a good one."

"John. A Bible study in John. What else?"

No Visible Scars

"It's on Wednesday nights from six o'clock to eight. So you can tell Nate that I'll pick you up at five thirty. You promise to make him a nice supper and put it in the fridge or the crock pot or whatever, so he'll feel taken care of and all that stuff."

Abigail nodded and leaned forward. "Yeah. That's good. What else?"

"I'll have you home by eight thirty. And it's only for eight weeks. And...it's free. Tell him it's at my church and it's free. That way, he won't know that I paid for you. Sound good?"

"Yes. What else?"

"That's it. Now, pretend I'm Nate. What do you say?"

Abigail cleared her throat and massaged her neck. Uncertainty began to lay its heavy burden on her shoulders. But who could deny Cassie's warm chestnut eyes and that friendly smile with a bit of mustard in the corner of her mouth? "Okay. Here I go. 'Nate...dear...uhm....'"

Cassie reached for Abigail's hand and patted it. "Yes, dear?"

"Well...you see...Cassie and I want to know if you'll let me go to...."

"Stop! '*Let* you go?' You're not asking his permission. You're telling him what we're doing."

"Oh. Sorry. I'm not very good at this."

"Here. Let me write it out. Then you can memorize it. Will that help?"

"Sure. I think so."

Cassie rummaged around in her bag for some paper while Abigail breathed deeply to stop her heart's thumping. If she was a basket case while practicing, how in the world could she lie in a convincing way?

Cassie wrote quickly on her blue Vera Bradley Post-it-note, then handed it to Abigail. "Okay, read it to me slowly, and say it like you mean it."

Abigail finished the last of her chai, then cleared her throat. She held out the sticky note and tried to keep her voice from shaking. "'Nate, dear, Cassie and I are going to a Bible study on Wednesday nights. She'll pick me up at five thirty and bring me home afterward, about eight thirty. I'll have your supper all fixed and ready for you. The study is free. It's at Cassie's church and we're studying the book of John.'"

"Good. Now do it again and this time, look at me and use more volume. Speaking loudly will help you feel more courageous."

Three times she repeated the words on the note, then looked at the rooster-shaped clock in the corner. "Uh-oh. Gotta' get back to work. Thanks so much, Cassie. I want to do this class with you, but I don't know if I can. Keep your fingers crossed."

"Right. I'll be saying lots of prayers. Send me an email that says, 'Yes' when you've done it. If I don't hear any different from you, I'll pick you up Wednesday night."

She kissed Cassie on the cheek, then hurried to her car.

No Visible Scars

All the way back to the office, Abigail practiced. On her way into the building, she crumpled up the sticky note and tossed it into the chrome trash can.

She walked into the Villas Corporate office and found Samuel, David and Nate near her work space. Nate glanced at the clock on the wall which showed two minutes after one. "Traffic," she said before he could complain.

David pulled out his iPhone and checked messages. Samuel smiled sweetly. "Here is the one person who keeps this organization running smoothly. How is your day going?"

"Fine. Thanks. In fact, I just met my friend for lunch." She suddenly realized the safety present in the room. "My friend Cassie and I…we've decided to go to a Bible study together on Wednesday nights, starting this week. The book of John, at her church. Five thirty. She'll pick me up. It's free."

She knew Samuel didn't need all that information, and she was totally surprised when it tumbled out of her mouth. Nate's left eyebrow raised, but she decided to focus on Samuel. She would have to answer to Nate later. But for now, she would use the physical presence of the other men to diffuse whatever her husband might say.

"A women's Bible study, you know," she repeated, "after work, on Wednesdays."

"What a wonderful idea!" Samuel said. "My wife goes to a weekly study and often tells me what she has learned. It's fascinating. Good for you." He turned toward

Nate. "You have a wonderful woman here, Nathan. I hope you realize that."

"Yes, sir. Indeed."

She knew Nate was trying to brown nose Samuel. As president of the board of directors, Samuel wanted all his employees and the entire organization to follow the highest of ethical and moral standards. That principle showed up in the people he and the board hired and also in the employees they let go. They wanted the Villas de Comfort to represent a quality organization for the residents who lived there and the families who paid the bills.

Ethical and moral standards. But she had just lied to her husband. Would her underlying motive, to learn something new that might change her life, justify the means? Was it okay to deceive her husband in order to save herself?

The men sauntered toward Nate's office. Abigail powered up her computer, watched the screen saver dance into life and quickly sent an email to Cassie. "YES," she typed, then hoped she hadn't just made the biggest mistake of her life.

❧❧❧

True to form, Nate grilled her that night. "What's this thing you and Cass are going to? Some kind of study on the book of John?"

Instead of trying to think of more lies, she repeated the words she had memorized earlier. "At Cassie's church. Wednesday nights. It's free, and she'll pick me up at 5:30."

"Yeah, I heard you the first time. Why can't you go to a study at our church? I'm a deacon, for Pete's sake.

What's the big deal about Cassie's church? How would it look if a deacon's wife goes to a different church for a Bible study? I don't like it."

"No one at our church needs to know about it. And Samuel liked the idea. Besides, it's free and Cassie will pick me up at 5:30...on Wednesdays."The mention of Samuel's name might give her some leverage.

Nate tapped his pointer finger on the granite counter top. "You already said that. Stop being stupid and repeating yourself. I'm going to think about this. Maybe I'll call Cass myself and look into it or talk to her dumb husband, that landscaping guy. I wonder what he thinks about his wife gallivanting off in the middle of the week."

She knew exactly what Rick thought. He would totally support Cassie. Lucky girl.

Memorizing info might be a good idea for the future, just in case she ever needed to lie again. For now, she was grateful for Cassie and her sticky note idea. This time, the tactic seemed to work.

She fed Nate one of his favorite meals—baked macaroni and cheese, then rubbed his feet until he relaxed enough to fall asleep in his recliner. Maybe this was actually going to happen. For the first time in forever, she felt a sliver of hope.

No Visible Scars

CHAPTER FIVE

Wednesday night, Cassie pulled up in her green SUV. Abigail climbed into the front seat, buckled her seat belt and exhaled a long breath. "I feel like I'm running away. Scared and excited at the same time."

Cassie giggled. "Let's consider it more of running toward something. Isn't this fun?"

"Not yet, but maybe it will be later."

Cassie expertly wound her way through the traffic on I-35, chatting the whole time about how she felt like a million bucks. "None of that nasty morning sickness today," she said. "Maybe I'm done with it."

Abigail smiled and watched for police cars in hidden places, her role when she drove with Nate. Warn him about cops. Don't let him get caught, just in case he was speeding. It wouldn't look good for a church deacon and a corporate leader to have his name on any police records. If he got a ticket, it would be her fault. Always her fault.

They pulled up to the Hope Gathering, a brick-fronted building with green shrubs and a Japanese maple that draped the left side of the building. A beautiful atmosphere inside, different from what Abigail expected in the artsy section of Westport.

Whoever designed this place knew about women. Comfy eggplant-colored love seats anchored the room. A crystal vase full of white roses sat on a mahogany end table. A bowl of Hershey's kisses next to a box of Kleenex invited any chocoholics who might be present. Several floor lamps reflected warm light. The room filled with women who clustered around an oval dining table, plastered name tags above their right boobs and seated themselves on the love seats, rockers or other comfy chairs.

As Abigail finished writing her name, she felt a tap on her shoulder. She turned and looked into the friendliest brown eyes she had ever seen. A woman slightly taller held out her hand. "I'm Jubilee," she said, "the facilitator of our Life Limits Class. Welcome."

She returned the handshake with a slight grin. "Thank you. I'm Abigail. This is a beautiful place. It feels…I don't know…sort of…safe."

Jubilee smiled widely. "So many women say that about our Hope Gathering. We work hard to make it safe and comfortable."

Abigail nodded. "I really like your hair."

"Thank you." Jubilee fluffed her silvery white hair, then pointed to a solid black patch beside the part on the left. "I'll bet you're wondering about this funny color right here."

Abigail nodded. "It's…unique," she said, hoping she wasn't offensive.

"The story behind it, and don't you know there's always a story behind everything that happens. Anyway, seven years ago, I was diagnosed with breast cancer and I had a mastectomy. By the way, it's the one on the left.

No Visible Scars

People always look at my chest to figure it out, so I've decided to just tell them."

Abigail felt herself flush. Sure enough, when Jubilee said "mastectomy," she immediately looked at Jubilee's chest, wondering which breast had been taken. "Sorry," she whispered.

"It's a natural response. Nothing for you to be sorry about. Anyway, after the chemo, my new hair came in snow white except for this one streak of my original black. I guess that patch didn't get the memo."

Jubilee laughed. Her eyes sparkled with the fresh joy of a woman who had not only survived a brutal disease but also conquered fear.

"I'm sorry about your cancer."

Jubilee reached for Abigail's hand. "But you are not responsible for my cancer. Therefore, you don't need to be sorry. You will learn in our class that you are not responsible for a great many burdens you may have carried. Now, find a seat, please. We'll be starting soon."

Abigail crossed the room to join Cassie on one of the love seats.

Cassie was already deep in conversation with the woman beside her, an older woman maybe in her fifties who patted her reddish and slightly graying hair as it stood tall in the old-fashioned beehive style. She plopped a brown pillow behind her back. "Fibromyalgia," she explained. "My heated pillow helps the muscles relax."

Abigail picked up the tweed pillow on the sofa and pressed it to her chest. Thinking of her conversation with

Jubilee, she leaned toward Cassie and whispered, "I think I have a lot to learn."

Cassie patted her hand for reassurance. Abigail mentally repeated, *Don't say you're sorry. Not everything is your fault.* She already liked Jubilee. She couldn't remember the last time someone told her something *wasn't* her fault.

Jubilee passed out some papers, then seated herself in a sage green wing chair. "These are our ground rules," she said. "A reminder to you that even at Hope Gathering, we have boundaries. Our number one rule is that everything said in this room stays in this room. Confidentiality is of prime importance. In fact, I don't even need to know your last names. But I want you to be honest, to feel safe, so you can share anything. After tonight, our group will be closed. No other women will be allowed to join us so we can get to know each other and build on our group relationship."

Abigail glanced around the room. Eight women, nine, counting Jubilee. Various shapes and sizes. Various ages and races. Maybe here at the Hope Gathering, it wouldn't matter what she revealed about her life. Maybe these women and this incredible Jubilee person would help her learn how to set personal boundaries, how to be a good wife.

Cassie's warmth next to her provided a cozy presence as they listened to Jubilee describe more of the ground rules. This group felt like the beginning of something special, the chrysalis of a new life or at least a different way to approach her current life.

Jubilee continued. "This place is for women only, because we've learned women share more easily when men aren't present. We want you to have the freedom to speak whatever is on your mind and whatever is locked within your heart. So...another safety feature at Hope Gathering...no men allowed."

One of the women said, "Amen."

Several others giggled.

Abigail sighed. The tension in her shoulders eased.

"Now I'd like to tell you a bit about myself," Jubilee said. "I was born and raised in Kenya, then moved to the United States and became a citizen. I finished my education and earned my master's degree in counseling. I'm a licensed professional counselor, a mother of three and a grandmother. Five precious grandbabies and another on the way. I'm a breast cancer survivor. the one on the left."

Jubilee tossed several pictures onto the Berber carpet. Walls, fences, a graphic of a list of rules, a white picket fence surrounding a garden. "Which of these pictures represents boundaries?"

The older woman with the fibromyalgia spoke first. "Is this a trick question? Because every picture is a type of boundary."

"Correct," said Jubilee. "Which one would you choose for yourself? Go ahead everyone. Choose a picture."

Cassie quickly grabbed the picket fence scene while the other women reached toward the floor and chose pictures they wanted. Abigail waited until all the pictures were chosen except one. Then she reached down and picked up the photo of a barbed wire prison fence. Standing on the inside, the gray faces of prisoners stared out of the enclosure. Maybe criminals to be punished for their crimes or one of those historical photos of a Holocaust camp.

While she tried to concentrate on the meaning of boundaries and the prison fence, she felt akin to the men trapped inside the enclosure. She knew exactly how they felt and what they wanted. Whether criminals or imprisoned Jews, they sought freedom, a way out of the entrapment that swallowed their souls and forced them to obey whoever was in authority over them.

Maybe she was here to find a type of freedom. But she thought this Life Limits Class was about personal control, helping women understand it was okay to say, "No." Wasn't there a type of security while living inside the fence?

Of course, cruelty to humankind was always wrong, as illustrated in the picture. But what about the type of security Nate provided? He did, after all, pay the bills and gave her everything she needed. She had never gone to bed hungry. At least not physically hungry. No one had ever asked about the hunger of her soul.

Jubilee's soft voice interrupted Abigail's trailing thoughts. "Now, I want to hear from you. Let's go around the room, beginning here on my left." She smiled at the brunette seated next to her. "Tell us your name and why you're here. Then tell us why you chose your particular picture."

The brunette smiled. "I'm Amber, and I have three children under the age of five." Several women groaned. "I'm here because my kids are driving me crazy. I want to know the difference between loving my kids and disciplining them. I chose this stone wall as my picture because I'd like to lock my kids behind that wall until they grow up and know how to behave."

No Visible Scars

Next to Amber sat a woman with beautiful skin, straight black hair and petite features. "My name Ling Su. I come to learn English. I not understand this word 'boundaries.' You explain, please?"

"Certainly," said Jubilee. "Ling Su, we're so glad you've come. A boundary can be any type of enclosure that represents safety or marks how far anyone can step forward, such as the boundaries between countries. You probably had to obtain a visa to come here. Correct?"

Ling Su nodded. "Yes. Student visa for one year."

"Countries have rules and boundaries. You'll understand even more as we proceed through our study. And if you have a question about an English word or phrase, please feel free to ask."

Ling Su bowed slightly as the woman next to her waved her picture which illustrated a list: Rules of the House. "What I want to know," she said, "Oh, my name is Lydia, and I'll bet I'm the oldest and tiredest woman here."

Another round of giggles as Jubilee said, "Don't be so sure about that."

"Yeah, well…. I've got two adult kids who won't leave home. I've put them through school, paid for their cars and given them everything they need. My husband escapes every day to work, and I'm left making meals for these grown kids and keeping the house going when all I really want to do is lie down and sleep for a hundred years. I want to know how to kick these kids out of the house. Everything is out of control and that's why I'm here."

Ling Su looked a bit puzzled. Amber leaned over to her and whispered something. Ling Su nodded.

Abigail took a deep breath. She stared at the picture of the prisoners.

A younger woman, Kathy, wore a bright orange headband. She attended because she was studying to become a counselor and wanted to learn more about how to share boundaries with her clients.

The woman next to Kathy played with her brunette pony tail before she said, "I'm Missy." Then she grabbed the box of Kleenex on the end table as she told about her ex-husband and how she wished she had known more about boundaries before she married him. "The jerk," she said. "He definitely broke the boundaries of our marriage vows." She waved the picture of a closed door. "My boundary is that my heart is closed to future relationships, at least until I heal."

The woman with fibromyalgia massaged her neck with one hand, then showed her picture of a cattle corral. Inside the corral stood a group of cows with their calves, little white faces on dark brown bodies. "I'm Martha," said the woman, "and you'll have to excuse me because sometimes I won't be able to come. This darn fibromyalgia with its muscle pain sometimes keeps me home in bed. Anyway, I'm here because I want to know better ways to help people understand when I can't go places. I don't want to sound like I'm whining all the time. And I chose this picture because I like cows."

Jubilee smiled. "I like cows, too, Martha, and we certainly understand if you need to miss a class session because of illness. That goes for all of you. Those with little children, you may need to be absent some night because of your child's needs. Don't be afraid to set boundaries around

No Visible Scars

your attendance." Jubilee nodded toward Cassie. "Next, please."

Cassie showed her picture of the white picket fence. "We have something like this in our back yard, and I love it. We planted some dark purple iris along one area and last spring, we put in some day lilies. My husband runs a landscaping business, and he's one of those rare men who does all the honey-do jobs at home. His name is Rick and I'm Cassie. And I guess I'm here, because well...hmm...I wanted my friend to come." Cassie squeezed Abigail's hand. "I'm also pregnant and I want to learn any parenting rules that might be helpful. I don't feel like my life is out of control or anything. I just think it's fun to get to know everyone and spend time with other women."

Good old Cassie. She made everything seem easy. If she was in this class to support their friendship, then it was Abigail's duty to make the supreme effort and learn everything possible. Cassie had said this class might change her life. She certainly wanted that to happen.

Jubilee nodded, then looked at Abigail. "Next?"

She would think about it later and wonder what in the world caused her to say what she did. Maybe it was because she felt safe with Jubilee and the rest of the group. The promise of total confidentiality seemed like a warm blanket wrapped around her shoulders. Maybe she decided to speak the truth because she hoped to discover more about herself. She wanted to have the freedom of Cassie to express herself and the authenticity of Jubilee to be totally honest.

For whatever reason, she met Jubilee's gaze. She held up the picture and said, "I live in an emotional prison. I'm Abigail, and I'm here to escape from my husband."

⁂

Abigail fastened her seat belt and turned toward Cassie."I wasn't sure this Life Limits Class was really for me, but after just one night...I'm amazed. I'm learning stuff I never thought about. What was it Jubilee said, 'We're afraid to be authentic because of what the consequences might be?'"

"Deep stuff. Are you afraid of consequences?"

"Well, sure, sometimes. I mean, I want to step into a new life and be my authentic self, but how do I do that? Should I set more boundaries? And how in the world does that happen without consequences?"

Cassie turned on the ignition and pulled into traffic. "It's probably that action reaction thing. You know, for every action there's a reaction. Something like that. But the consequences don't always have to be bad, do they?"

Abigail shook her head. "I hope not. I certainly have a lot to learn. I really like this Jubilee person."

CHAPTER SIX

Something different was going on with Abby. Nate couldn't quite voice it or even picture the source of the problem, but it was obvious.

He first noticed it when she started going to that Bible study thing with Cass. She seemed happier somehow with a faraway look on her face, almost as if she moved within another world.

She carried herself differently, sort of more erect, more confident. Yes. That was the word he had been searching for. Abby seemed more confident, less timid and more willing to speak her mind. In fact, she was turning into a nag.

At work one day, she said, "I think we can find a more efficient way to record mileage reimbursements for the staff. Look at this idea I found online."

It *was* a good idea, but he didn't want Dave or Sam or any of the board members thinking his wife knew more than he. So he pulled her aside after their staff meeting and reminded her, "You're just the executive assistant. You have no right to tell us how to do business."

That seemed to settle her down for a while. But the next day, she brought up going back to school—again. He was so tired of that argument.

She twirled her hair and said, "I really want to finish my degree. It's my dream to teach little kids."

"Your dream? Don't you know dreams are fairy tales? Besides, your role as my wife is to support *my* goals and that means staying at your desk at the Villas. What good is it to finish a degree you'll never use? That would be a waste of time and money. Forget it."

She tried to argue later that night, but he threatened to cut off more of her allowance. She seemed to cower in her chair, which repulsed and delighted him at the same time.

He clenched his fists, but knew he would never hit her. He wasn't a thug, but she needed to be reminded of her place. "I don't know where you got the idea that you can keep arguing about this school thing. You know I'm the final authority in the home. Haven't you been listening in church?"

It was all Cassie's fault. She was the one who persuaded Abby to go to that Bible study. What kind of false doctrine were they teaching? Maybe some of those liberal ideas he had heard about at the last church convention.

He needed to protect Abby from any deception. Everyone knew women were easily deceived, ever since Eve screwed up everything in the Garden of Eden. It was up to the men to make sure women learned correctly and then lived out the truth. As a church deacon, he had the additional priority of making sure his home operated as a spiritual example.

No Visible Scars

She fixed his breakfast plate and started humming. "Why are you so happy?" he asked as he flipped open the paper she laid beside his place setting.

"Oh, I don't know. I guess because it's Wednesday and I'm going to Bible study with Cassie tonight. I'm learning so much, and the other women are fabulous."

"Yeah? So how many more weeks of this study do you have?"

"I don't know, but we've talked about a follow-up. It depends on Jubilee's schedule."

"Jubilee? Who's that?"

"She's the leader, the facilitator of the group. She's really great, and I admire her so much."

"Humph! So what kind of credentials does this Jubilee person have? She's not one of those liberals who thinks it's okay to ordain women, is she?"

Abby looked puzzled. "I don't know her politics or her religion, but she *is* a licensed counselor."

She walked to the fridge and pulled out a container of yogurt. She stuck a spoon in it, then dolloped a bit into her mouth. That pretty little mouth he fell in love with all those years ago. She still stirred him up. He didn't want anything or anyone to change her.

Now she was at the sink and humming again. Something was definitely wrong. "I don't like the idea of you doing another study with this Jubilee person and Cass. I want you home on Wednesday nights."

"That's not fair. You sometimes go places with David during the evenings, to check on the Villas or work on a new project. I don't have any friends other than Cassie, and

57

I really enjoy this group of women. It's only right that I have some time to myself during the week."

He glanced at his watch. "We'll discuss it later. It's time to get to work. For now, you can finish this study because you've already started it. But I'll have to look into it more carefully before I let you go to another one."

She held herself erect and looked straight at him. For a minute, he felt a shiver down his spine. "I'm a grown woman, Nate. Yes, I want your blessing and your agreement to continue with this group, but I can make up my own mind."

Her eyes grew big, as if she was surprised at what she had just said. He needed to squelch that pride right out of her. He slapped the paper on the table. "You're my wife, and you'll do what I say. Let's go."

Fortunately, she didn't hum as they drove to work. And the rest of the week, she seemed exceptionally quiet— just the way he wanted her to be.

※※※

They always walked in the church doors on time, because that's the way Nate operated. One Sunday, she had chatted with a woman in the bathroom, then joined Nate in their usual pew. "Where the heck have you been?" he whispered. "The worship team is already on the stage."

"Sorry," she said, wishing she could say, "What's the big deal?" She hated his compulsiveness almost as much as she hated herself for putting up with it. If only she could mirror the authenticity of Jubilee and tell Nate how she felt about everything he did. A deacon in the church—humph! A hypocrite, that's what he was.

Yet what was she, the wife who silently condoned his behaviors and lived in a cavern of fear. Afraid of him, but terrified of telling the truth, of living an authentic life, of letting the leadership of the church know about the dreadful life she lived. Who would believe her?

When tall, handsome and ambitious Nate courted her, she felt overwhelmed with excitement. In only four dates, she was certain he was the forever love of her life. She promised to love, honor and obey until death parted them.

But how many deaths would she have to endure?

Because she had met Jubilee and started learning about setting boundaries, she began to see the deception. Maybe it was time to become herself and move toward her dreams. The problem was, she didn't know who she was anymore. A fog of surrealism hung over her soul, wrapping her in giant question marks.

Perhaps Jubilee was right in the statement she made during class. "Sometimes discomfort becomes our comfort zone. We forget how to truly live because we've survived within the chaos so long."

She longed to escape. Yet the fear of escape was stronger than the dread of staying. A coward. That's what she was.

She tried to concentrate on what Pastor Dennis said. He invited his wife to join him at the pulpit. "We've just read from Ephesians chapter five, so I've asked my darling wife, Evelyn, to help me explain how a godly marriage works."

Spotlights focused on the couple. A flashing beam from the drum set to their right. Evelyn stood beside her husband, a lovely smile on her face. Abigail barely knew the pastor's wife, but she seemed nice enough. Pretty. Confident in her role.

Evelyn opened her Bible and read, "You wives must submit to your husbands' leadership in the same way you submit to the Lord. For a husband is in charge of his wife. You must willingly obey your husbands."

Pastor Dennis put his arm around her shoulder. "And do you believe that, honey?"

"Of course I do, although I'll admit it isn't always easy."

A few giggles in the sanctuary. Nate tapped his pointer finger on his open Bible, the Ephesians passage outlined in red.

Pastor Dennis nodded. "In the reality of our everyday world, shouldn't husbands and wives work better as a team? Can't they make joint decisions and pray about things together? Of course they can. Teamwork is essential. No husband wants an unhappy wife."

Evelyn nodded. Pastor Dennis continued, "But even on a team, somebody has to be the leader. Somebody has to be the coach, to steer the team to victory. It's very clear in this passage who is to lead—the man, of course. And who is to submit—the woman. Marriage works better when the woman is the helper rather than the leader."

Evelyn spoke up. "I know this sounds difficult, especially to some of you women who have leadership qualities. But trust me. When you truly learn how to submit and let your husband be the boss, your marriages will be so much better."

Abigail felt her stomach tighten. She rubbed it and tried to breathe slowly. She looked around the room and wondered if anyone had a dissenting opinion. Sure, it sounded right and probably that formula worked well for Pastor Dennis and Evelyn. But what if the husband demanded authority and used the Bible as his backup for cruelty?

Pastor Dennis continued as Evelyn exited the stage and took her place on the front row. "Other places in scripture make this principle clear. The books of Corinthians and Timothy both talk about the woman in the subservient role, even to the point of how she should dress and act. Women should never teach men. They are encouraged to be quiet and by their very sweetness, inspire their men to be better. In fact, women feel more secure when men take control."

Abigail was beginning to wonder if she needed a new definition of security. She used her bulletin as a fan, tried to cool some of the frustration warming her face.

The spotlights focused on the wooden cross, flanked by navy blue velvet cloth. Pastor Dennis concluded, "Remember, submission and sacrifice go together, but they always end in victory."

Sacrifice. A good word. Here she sat, submissively next to her husband as Pastor Dennis explained the finer points of the Pauline epistles. She had sacrificed her dream for her husband's needs. But somehow, she didn't feel victorious.

Where were Paul's answers for her? Was there a passage of instruction for how to act when your husband calls you a freak, when he pulls out your hair, when he dares you to deny him nightly pleasures even when you grit your teeth to endure it? Her stomach tightened again. She decided to hate Paul.

Nate grasped her hand. He squeezed so hard, her wedding band pressed into the adjoining fingers. Her hand felt as small as her personhood.

She did not join in the final "Amen."Instead, she whispered to God the only prayer she thought might work. *Help me, please.*

Maybe she should talk to Pastor Dennis and ask for clarification. Surely he could give her some pointers. His wife seemed happy enough. They had figured out how to make their relationship work. At least, she could give Pastor Dennis and the church a chance.

CHAPTER SEVEN

Abigail parked in the church lot. Was this the dumbest thing she had ever done in her life? But she had made the appointment with Pastor Dennis, after his big sermon about marital teamwork. If she cancelled now, he would think she was one of those women who couldn't make up her mind. She had already cancelled two previous appointments, chickened out at the last minute.

No. This time she would go through with it. She needed to know about the spiritual boundaries in marriage and what God expected of her.

She locked the car, then shoved the key into her coat pocket. Her fingers edged onto a piece of paper, and she pulled it out. A business card, one corner turned down and the rest of it smudged with coat fuzz. Officer Tamara. How long had it been—several months? That nice policewoman who couldn't help because Abigail had never returned to the station, never called 9-1-1.

This time she would go to a higher authority. Pastors were supposed to know how to counsel couples and help people find the answers to life. On the way into the building, she tossed Officer Tamara's card in the trash.

No Visible Scars

In the cozy office, the church secretary smiled and offered coffee. Abigail shook her head. She unzipped her purse and looked for a breath mint. Couldn't find one. Zipped it up again.

Pastor Dennis concentrated on his phone call. Then he waved and mouthed, "Come in." His desk littered with paper. His Bible open. Obviously working on the next sermon. A picture of his loving family on vacation with the banner of Walt Disney World in the background.

"Sure Ed, I'll come visit your wife as soon as I finish with an appointment. What's her room number again? Saint Luke's, right?" He scribbled on a Post-it note. "And tell her I'll be praying for her. For you, too, Ed."

He placed the receiver in its cradle, then leaned forward, his full attention on Abigail. "What can I do ya' for? What brings you in to see me?"

She cleared her throat. "Sorry to bother you on such a busy day." She sighed. "It's a marital problem. We probably need couples counseling, but Nate won't hear of it. I've asked him several times and he just says, 'Why mess with something good?' But I think we have a problem, and I don't know how to fix it."

"Hmm. Nate hasn't indicated anything to me. I just saw him at the deacons' meeting this week, and he seemed happy. He said business is going well."

"Oh, it is. It's not the business that's the problem. It's more about his attitude." She unzipped her purse, then zipped it closed. Twice.

Pastor Dennis crossed his arms. "For instance? Can you give me an example?"

"How detailed do you want me to be?"

"Well, if you don't tell me the honest truth, I won't know how to help."

She took a deep breath. "All right. But I have to tell you this isn't something new. It's been going on for a while, but it seems to be ... I don't know ... escalating. More often and more cutting remarks. Nate calls me names and shuts me down when I try to express my opinion about anything. He laughs at me if I disagree with him, calls me things like 'insipid.' Much of the time we barely communicate. The rest of the time I feel like his slave. Work bleeds into home. I'm his executive assistant, you know, at the Villas."She dug her fingernails into her fists, willing herself not to cry.

"Anything else?" he asked.

Probably better not to tell him about the forceful sex. It was too embarrassing. "I've tried everything I know to make things better. At work, I do everything Nate asks me to do. At home, I do the same. Lately, I've tried some extra things. Made his favorite meal at least once a week. Tried not to disagree with him when he yells at the politicians on the TV."

Pastor Dennis grinned. "That must be difficult."

"I just don't know what to do anymore."

He shuffled some of the papers on his desk, then fiddled with a paper clip. "Okay. Let's talk this through."He closed his eyes for a moment.

She watched him and fidgeted with her purse. Probably praying. Yep. His lips moved.

When he looked up, she thought the worry lines in his forehead were deeper than before. Poor guy. He probably

No Visible Scars

heard lots of sad stories every day and still needed to visit someone in the hospital after he finished with her.

"Abigail, are you involved in any of the women's ministries here at the church?"

"No. I don't have time. Not with the work at the Villas and our social calendar and everything. Nate doesn't like me to spend a lot of evenings without him."

"Do you have any close friends?"

"Just Cassie, but she doesn't go to this church."

"And...just to clarify...Nate hasn't hit you, has he? No bruises or scars?"

"No. He hasn't hit me." No need to tell Pastor Dennis about the broken finger or the yanking of her hair.

"Okay. That's good." He reached into a drawer and pulled out a folder. "I'm going to give you a copy of an excellent article. It talks about how wives should submit to their husbands and what a difference it makes in the marriage. The author of this article is writing from personal experience."

He handed several pages to her. "Then I would suggest that you begin praying blessings for your husband and try to remember how you fell in love with him in the first place. Concentrate on the positives rather than the negatives. I also want you to know the deacons and I are studying a book together about how to honor our wives, how to love them more. Nate will be part of that discussion at our monthly meetings. And remember, God loves you. He wants you to be involved with the church and have a healthy marriage. I suggest that you join one of the ladies' Bible studies. Of course, if you need a referral to a woman counselor, the church secretary can give you a name and number."

She briefly scanned the article in her hands, then looked at her pastor. Surely he had more to add.

He cleared his throat. "I cannot imagine Nate will ever physically hurt you, and I suspect the mental strain of his business is, as you say, bleeding over into the home. If he agrees to couples counseling, I will be happy to meet with the two of you."

Maybe she should have gone back to Officer Tamara after all. She stood and walked toward the door. "Thank you for your time," she said without looking back.

"Abigail." Pastor Dennis walked around his desk and put his hand on her shoulder. "I'll be praying for you."

She muttered another "Thank you," but she felt numb. Devalued. Without another word, she walked out of the office, ignoring the secretary's, "Have a nice day."

She stumbled out the exit door, then ran across the lot to her car, fumbling in her purse. She emptied her purse on the car's hood. No keys. Checked her coat pocket. There. She grabbed her billfold, her lipstick and a half-eaten Milky Way, then jammed them back into her purse. A wad of Kleenex blew away.

Inside the car, she beat on the steering wheel. "Submit? That's supposed to solve the problem? Isn't that what I've been doing all along?"

She watched as Pastor Dennis left the building and hurried to his car, probably on his way to that hospital visit. He was her pastor and she respected him, but he obviously didn't know how to help her. Yeah, he could pray for her, but she wasn't going to spill her guts in his office. Never again.

※※※

The following Wednesday, Martha brought up the subject of victim mentality. She rearranged her heated pillow to a spot behind her, then sighed.

"Do you want to elaborate on that topic, Martha?" Jubilee leaned forward in her chair, a kind expression on her face.

"Sure. I don't mind, and I'll be the first to confess that I have trouble setting boundaries. I struggle to say, 'No' to anybody. I kind of feel like I deserve to be tromped on by others. I have a hard time fighting for myself and even sometimes saying what I think, believe it or not."

Amber laughed, then snorted, which caused everyone else to laugh. Abigail studied her fingernails. It was probably time to schedule a manicure. Nate always wanted her to look professional at the office. Only French tips. Nothing too scandalous. No bright colors.

"Go ahead, Martha," Jubilee urged. "Finish your thought."

"Well, I'm just sayin' that lots of little girls aren't allowed to grow up and be who they want to be. And that kind of sets us up for failure. That whole attitude about women being second best keeps us from being confident and setting healthy boundaries. Am I right?"

Jubilee nodded. "We often mirror in adulthood the experiences of childhood."

Amber held up her hand. "It happened to me that way. I grew up with five brothers, and they got to do everything they wanted. I wanted to be outside playing sports, but my parents made me stay inside, to help Mom cook and clean. Do you think I have trouble with my kids because I don't want to act like my parents? Maybe that's part of it. I don't want to set too strict of boundaries with them because I don't want to squelch who they are. Hey! A breakthrough!"

Martha and Cassie clapped. Jubilee looked around the room at the group. "What do the rest of you think?"

Cassie shook her head. "I can't really respond. My childhood was pretty happy." She addressed Amber. "I'm sorry that happened to you."

Missy nodded. "In our sorority, we talked about victimization all the time. Most of us had been through it, some sort of abuse at home, and some of the girls had been raped on campus. It was really scary. We were told to always travel in groups or at least with a friend. I still carry my can of pepper spray."

"Good idea," said Jubilee. "It's wise to know how to protect yourselves. The community college has an excellent program on self-defense, and I can give you that information after class.

It's also common that women who have been abused as children will often choose abusive men to marry. Or they try to compensate for some type of childhood unhappiness and end up with unhealthy relationships.

"Since we've touched on the topic of self defense and victimization, let me show you something interesting."

Jubilee stood. "Last year, I took a class for women on how to defend ourselves. Martha, would you help me, please?"

Martha stood and joined Jubilee in the center of the room. "Am I the good guy or the bad guy?"

"The bad guy. Now, you'll notice my assailant is taller than I am. I would guess she is also stronger, so she has the advantage. Martha, come closer to me and place your hands around my throat."

"Lordy!" said Cassie.

Jubilee continued. "The choke hold is one of the most difficult to break, because we think we can kick our way out of it or somehow break the hold of this person who is stronger. But within seconds, the attacker can crush your windpipe. So here's what we should do."

While Martha pretended to choke her, Jubilee clasped her hands together. "Bring your clenched hands up toward the attacker's chin. The force of coming from below will surprise him and as you jar his chin, as hard as you can, that will snap his head back and break the force of his hands on your neck."

Jubilee illustrated the upward thrust several times. Martha played along by staggering backward and yelling, "Ouch! She got me!"

"Thank you, Martha. I hope none of you ever has to use this example. But if you do, and after you have broken the choke hold of your attacker, don't stand around and watch him fall down or wait to see what happens. Run like a bat out of hell."

Everyone clapped and congratulated Martha on playing an excellent bad guy. Jubilee smoothly segued into a discussion about the class schedule. Several of the women needed to prepare for spring break, so Jubilee decided to cancel the class for the next week.

"However," she said as she stacked her papers on her lap. "I've set aside Wednesday evenings for this group, so my time is free. If any of you would like to speak with me individually, let me know. I'm available, and there's no extra charge."

Abigail thought about the possibility of meeting with Jubilee. Nate would never know she and Cassie had a night away from their pretend Bible study. Maybe it would help to let Jubilee know how confused she was about setting boundaries within a Christian marriage. She had already tried Pastor Dennis and Officer Tamara. Maybe this was a step in the right direction.

While the other women took a bathroom break and feasted on the granola bars Missy brought, Abigail searched in her purse. She sighed.

Cassie leaned toward her. "What do you need, friend?"

"A small piece of paper to leave a note for Jubilee."

"Got it." Cassie reached into her bag and brought out a packet of blue and grey Post-it-notes. "Keep the pack. I've got more at home."

Abigail wrote, "I would like to talk to you next week, on our free night." Then she stood up and passed the note to Jubilee.

Jubilee nodded, then smiled at Abigail. She wrote on the note and passed it back. "I'll see you next week at six o'clock."

It proved easier than Abigail imagined to leave the house that Wednesday night as Nate came home drunk. He passed out on the sofa without explaining why he had been drinking or how he managed to drive himself home.

She left him a note. "I'm at Bible study. Your supper is in the crock pot, broccoli and cheesy rice. Hope you like it. Driving myself tonight. See you later."

As she backed out of the garage, she felt as if a twenty-pound burden had lifted from her shoulders. Even the headache triggered by a busy day at the office seemed to ease. She swallowed another Tylenol, put her car into drive and headed toward Westport.

CHAPTER EIGHT

Abigail settled into a chair across from Jubilee. She grabbed a pillow and held it close. "You know how we talked last week about that victim mentality stuff? Well, I'm wondering about that. Did I choose to marry Nate because of the sadness of my childhood?"

"Go on," said Jubilee, her brown eyes compassionate. The white hair above her face an accessory, along with that one streak of black rebellion. "What happened to you that was so sad?"

"It was more of my mother's sadness, I guess, because I was a baby when my father left. We had to live with my grandparents for a while, and Grandpa was so...downright mean. He yelled at Mama, told her she was a loser. She never fought back, but she protected me. Sometimes he would spank me with a belt so hard it left welts, all because I spilled my milk or didn't clean my plate. Then Mama would come between Grandpa and me. One time, he slapped her so hard, her mouth started bleeding."

Abigail shook her head and tried to clear the memories. She reached for a Kleenex and blew her nose. "I've never told anyone that story. I feel like a giant rock on my heart just lifted."

"Thank you," said Jubilee, "for being so brave and trusting me with your story. What did your mother do after that horrible attack?"

"That night, after we heard Grandpa snoring, we threw our clothes in paper sacks and left. Mama called it an adventure. I think I was about four at the time, not in school yet. We stayed that night at the YWCA. I remember because Mama helped me sound out the letters on the front of the building. After we settled in our room, we took a bubble bath in the hallway bathroom. Mama wanted me to feel better. I loved bubbles."

For a moment, Abigail disappeared back into that bathroom with the turquoise tub and its matching toilet. Mama helped her into the bubbly water and gently rubbed her back with the washcloth.

Then Mama faded into Jubilee and the turquoise tub became the chair where she sat. She crossed her legs and set the pillow on her lap. "Mama found a job as a waitress and by the time I started school, we lived in a one-bedroom apartment above a garage. We never went back to see my grandparents, and that made me sad. I loved my grandmother, but she was afraid of Grandpa, too."

Jubilee seemed to process the information for a while. "And you never connected with your father?"

"No, he completely disappeared from the picture." Abigail sighed. "Mama worked hard and saved every penny. She kept telling me, 'Stay away from the boys. Get your education. Then you'll have better choices in life.' She was right. I studied hard and never dated during high school.

No Visible Scars

Nate was my first serious boyfriend, and now...I think he's becoming my grandpa." She gasped as the truth spilled out.

Jubilee nodded. "Sometimes women compensate for the loss of a father. They latch onto the first man who shows them any kindness."

"Yeah, that was Nate. He listened to me, bought me little treats, invited me for coffee and meals at the best restaurants. He seemed so kind and gentle—back then."

"So what are you doing now, Abigail, to set healthy boundaries and protect your heart? Remember one of the principles in our Life Limits Class: When we have a change of heart, it precedes some type of action."

She shook her head. "I know that's true, but I'm not ready to do anything yet. Nate controls all the money. I didn't finish my education. I don't want to end up in a tiny apartment, working so hard like Mama. Making a life-changing decision requires too much energy." She sighed deeply.

"I understand," Jubilee answered, kindness in her voice. "Still, not making a decision is also deciding on a course of action, of staying unhappy and letting the situation remain the same."

Abigail thought for a moment. "I'm kind of wondering...."

"What? What do you wonder about?"

"Well...why didn't God do something? Why did he allow this whole mess to happen? I was so naïve and didn't know anything about setting personal or social limitations. Then Nate came along. Why didn't God warn me? I don't get it."

Jubilee shook her head. "That's the question of the ages. Why does God allow suffering? I can't answer that and scholars who are smarter than I don't know how to answer it either. With some questions in life, we just have to leave the reasons with God. Then we do the best we can to find healing and hope. Good old Job in the Bible probably said it best. His philosophy was 'No matter what happens, I'll trust God.'"

Abigail nodded. "Yeah, I guess that covers everything, but it's not easy to trust God to work it all out."

"Certainly not. And we also need to do our part toward healing, just as you're doing now by telling the truth about what happened. Admitting the truth is the first and most important step."

Abigail studied her fingernails. A mourning dove warbled outside the window and she smiled. "I sometimes see mourning doves in our back yard. They make a fluttering sound when they fly away."

Jubilee's brown eyes brightened. "Maybe God sent that dove as a reminder to you."

"A reminder? Of what?"

"Mourning. That he grieves with you for what has happened. That he also hates the evil and suffering in this world. That he cares for you and wants to comfort you. Do you think that's possible?"

"I guess. Maybe. It's a nice thought." Abigail wiped a tear that meandered down her cheek.

Jubilee spoke softly, then smiled as the mourning dove warbled again. "So where do we go from here? How can I help you now?"

No Visible Scars

"What I want to know is this…how I can set personal boundaries with my husband when he's…well … he's so difficult to live with?"

"Has he ever hit you?"

"Oh, no. It's mostly just the words he uses and the way he treats me. I guess he sort of beats me up with his mouth. His tongue is his favorite weapon. I know he can't help himself, but I can't seem to do anything about it. My shoulders and my neck hurt all the time. Tension, I guess.

"I never get to make my own choices, and I really don't know what I would choose if I had that much freedom. It's kind of hard for me to make decisions, because I'm afraid of what Nate's reaction will be."

Jubilee touched Abigail's hand. "I'm so glad you're coming to our class. We've talked about making small changes gradually, tiny first steps. Would you like to consider an additional counseling session every week? We could work on this together."

Abigail shook her head. "Nate would never agree to that. He thinks counseling is for weak people. No. I'll keep coming to class with Cassie and see how everything plays out. But thank you for listening. I feel better now."

The phone rang, and Jubilee looked at the caller ID. "My next client is here." She gave Abigail some pamphlets about safe places for women and a phone number she could call, "Just in case you need help. And please remember…I'm available if you want to talk again."

"Sure. Thanks."

On her way home, Abigail stopped at Sonic, suddenly hungry for cheese tots and a cherry limeade. She browsed through the pamphlets that described some of the symptoms of domestic abuse: threats, controlling behaviors, demanding submissiveness. If she had a pen, she could have checked off at least ten of the symptoms as adjectives to describe her life.

She could ask Cassie to keep the pamphlets in a safe place, but it was too late now to drive to Cassie's house and then back home. Nate would wonder why she was walking in the door so much later than usual.

She couldn't risk it. She drove past the trash bin at Sonic and tossed in the pamphlets. Even though she wanted to read more of the information, she felt proud of herself for making some decisions on her own. She had set up this session with Jubilee and spoken her truth. She had decided not to keep the pamphlets. In a way, she was protecting herself from Nate's anger and that felt good.

Married yet according to that list, she was abused. Controlled yet trying to set healthy boundaries. Her thumb played with the back of her wedding ring. Shackled to an abuser forever and feeling every bit like Nate's victim.

CHAPTER NINE

"Bring some of your brownies to the office today," Nate said. "We have a big meeting with Sam, and we have to impress him." He slid into his chair at their breakfast table.

Abigail packed eight brownies in a Tupperware container, knowing David would also want some. Nate might eat a couple, just to please Samuel. He would do anything to get on Samuel's good side and hopefully become the next CEO of the Villas de Comfort.

Nate sipped from his "I'm Number One" coffee cup, then nodded as Abigail offered to top it off. "Sam really needs to make a decision soon," he said. "Saul isn't working out like we hoped. He's failed miserably at marketing and can't seem to attract the right residents."

Abigail spooned a dollop of her peach yogurt on top of a sliced banana. "What do the perfect residents look like?"

"People who want a beautiful place to live out their final years but also have the capital to afford the very best. Our tagline, 'The Best Place for Senior Living' reinforces that concept, and I'm the one who came up with it. I hope Sam remembers that fact. Maybe you can give him a gentle hint today. He likes you. Remind him I'm the best man for the job."

"How am I supposed to do that?"

He scowled. "Use your brain, Abby. Hand him a brownie and say how much you appreciate everything I add to the company. Remind him how hard I work. I'm due for a promotion and a raise. It's high time Sam and the board chose the best asset for the company. That would be me."

On one level, she was proud of Nate's work at the Villas. He worked hard to make older people more comfortable in their latter years, and he made the company look good. Whenever he met with any of the elderly residents, he seemed to connect with them. Nate probably *was* the right choice for the CEO position.

She could barely tolerate Saul. An athletic man in his sixties with a dark head of hair still thick and wavy, Saul acted like a dictator. When he occasionally breezed into the office, he expected all his work stacked neatly on his desk in alphabetical order, ready for his signature on important documents. Abigail supplied everything he needed, but hated the way he leered at her underneath the rim of his reading glasses. She dealt with enough male ego at home.

She shivered and finished rinsing off the breakfast dishes. Time to focus on the day's work.

An hour later, Nate stood over her desk, checking her appointment ledger just as David walked in. Nate pointed at Abigail's notation. "Call the vendor that's scheduled for ten o'clock and reschedule. I think we'll be in session with Sam longer than we originally planned."

"Really?" asked David. "I thought it was supposed to be a summary of the last board meeting. Something else going on?"

"Who knows? We'll find out soon enough. I imagine Sam will be on task, and you know he doesn't like to waste any time. Who knows what Saul will bring up." Nate's pointer finger tapped against Abigail's ledger.

David reached for the Tupperware container on the corner of her desk. "Umm...brownies?"

She nodded. "But let's wait until Samuel gets here. Then I'll put them on a nice platter in the conference room."

"Aw, come on. Can't I have just one?" David pleaded.

She wasn't sure what to do. Of course, it was all right for David to eat one of her treats, but she saw Nate's frown. She waited for his permission.

He grabbed the container and pushed it toward the back of her desk. "Forget it, Dave. You can have one later. Geez, you're just like a little kid. We need to get busy and make sure everything's ready for the meeting. Abby, get those papers I told you about copied and stacked in the conference room." He hurried back to his office.

"Yes, sir," she replied, then stifled a giggle as David grabbed the Tupperware container, sneaked his hand under the lid and pulled out a brownie.

"I'll make sure this stays safe with me until the meeting starts," he said.

She carried the printed copies to the conference room table, then powered up the Keurig coffee maker and piled plenty of K-cups in the basket next to it. David would choose the hazelnut while Nate drank only the dark roast. Samuel sometimes indulged in a mocha or maybe a green tea. If Saul came he might ask her to brew something special for him.

She arranged the brownies on a crystal platter then found a knife to cut them into smaller squares. If only she could easily square off her own life, erase all the broken pieces and somehow make life enjoyable.

As she settled at her desk again, Michele strolled in, her newest Coach bag a bright silver accessory to her eggplant purple dress. Abigail felt like a plain sparrow, sharing the same room with a colorful peacock.

"Is David here yet?" Michele reached up to swipe her bangs away from her eyes. Her beautifully manicured nails sported the latest of the blue polishes.

Before Abigail could page him, David walked out of his office. "I thought I heard your voice, babe," he said as he planted a kiss on Michele's cheek. "Your dad isn't here yet, but you and I can have some coffee together. And..." he winked at Abigail, "We have some wonderful brownies, just waiting to be eaten."

"Are you kidding?" Michele brushed against David's chest."You know I'm on a no- carbs diet this month. Gotta' get ready for bikini season."

"Oh, yeah. I'm lookin' forward to that." David grasped Michele's hand and they sauntered back to his office.

Abigail clicked onto the internet and read the morning news. Nate wanted her to stay up
to date on current events, especially anything that might apply to assisted living facilities. He wanted a report when any of their sites experienced a communications problem or a power outage from a storm or especially a runaway. Silver Alerts had to be immediately filtered back through Nate so

he could reduce any collateral damage. She had to admit he was good at his job. It was only relationships where he stunk. Or maybe, just his relationship with her.

She fired off an email to Cassie. "Having an okay day," she wrote. "President of the board is coming soon. What about you?"

Cassie answered back. "Feeling rotten. Eating crackers and dry Cheerios."

"Sorry. Wish I could help."

"You can't, but thanks. Did you have a good meeting with Jubilee on Wednesday?"

Abigail hesitated, her hands on the keyboard. She thought for a moment, then sipped a bit of her English Breakfast tea. "Good on one hand. On the other, kind of hard to talk about things."

"Like peeling an onion," Cassie wrote back. "Each layer important, but lots of tears."

They emailed back and forth and scheduled their next coffee date. Then Abigail carefully deleted all the personal emails. No use giving Nate any more ammunition. She never knew when he might check her computer to make sure she used her time well. And she certainly didn't want him to know she had scheduled an extra session with Jubilee.

Samuel and Saul arrived at the same time, so she notified Nate and David. Michele followed David out of his office and gracefully crossed the room to greet her father.

"Hi, Daddy. I'll meet you for lunch at Houlihan's on the Plaza, okay?"

Saul kissed Michele's hand. "Right. See you at noon in our usual booth." Michele breezed out, leaving a whiff of her cologne in the reception area.

"Man!" said David, grinning at Michele's retreating form.

Saul frowned at him.

As the men filed into the conference room, Abigail followed and readied everything for the meeting. She handed each of them a folder she had prepared with monthly stats and the year-to-date summary. The proposal for a new Villa in Pennsylvania was neatly typed and placed on the right side, second page.

Nate was picky about the placement of items. "The most important page is on the right," he said when she once tried to place the logo page on the left. "Most people look to the right side first."

Although she knew the men could operate the Keurig themselves, she offered to brew their drinks for them. Sure enough, David chose hazelnut, Nate, the dark roast and today, Samuel chose green tea. Saul decided he wanted only water, so she hurried to the office break room and found a Perrier cooling on the second shelf of the fridge.

"I don't know what we would do without you," Samuel said as she passed the platter of brownies to him. "You always make everything perfect." He bit into a brownie. "Wonderful."

"Thank you, sir."

Nate cleared his throat. "I think we have everything we need, Abby. Close the door behind you."

No Visible Scars

She obeyed, careful to not make a sound as she gently closed the door. Then she whispered on her way back to her desk, "Abigail. My name is Abigail. Stop calling me Abby."

It felt good to speak it to herself. Maybe it was time to set a personal boundary and demand she be called by her real name.

※※※

"Hey, Abby, I figured out...new name for you."

It was no surprise when Nate came home after work and made himself a screw driver. He spilled some of the orange juice on the floor, a sticky mess she cleaned up. Then he followed her around the kitchen, complaining and drinking more vodka.

She emptied out the dishwasher. Placed the dishes in the cabinets. All white dishes. Just as Nate liked them.

He stood at her elbow. "Stupid old Sam. Stupid board of directors. Don't know wha' they're doin'. Givin' that old Saul 'nother chance."

Abigail cringed as she listened to Nate's blubbering. "Don't 'preciate all I do. I got lots o' ideas. Gonna' show 'em, bet your bottom dollar."

She poured another cup of black coffee and offered it to him. "Don't want," he said, shoving her hand away. Some of the coffee sloshed over and burned her hand. She hurried to the sink to run cold water on it.

He stumbled toward the den and yelled, "I got yer new name. Wanta' hear? Abscess. That's what. Get it? Starts with Ab, but Abscess. Putrid. Smelly. Gross. That's what I call you now."He belched.

She gritted her teeth as she stood at the sink. "My name is Abigail," she said, her throat raw. "Do not call me Abby or Abscess or anything else. I am Abigail."

"Wha...? Whaddya' say?"

He shuffled back into the kitchen. She knew he was drunk enough he wouldn't understand what she had said. On the other hand, maybe this was the perfect opportunity to set a boundary and demand more respect.

She cleared her throat and turned to face him. He held on to the kitchen table for support. "I said, 'My name is Abigail.' I am not an abscess, and...I also don't like the nickname Abby. Do not call me that again."
She turned back toward the faucet. When she heard a shuffling sound, she turned around. He grabbed a bottle of Merlot from the wine rack and stumbled back to the den.

"Abscess...that's what," he mumbled.

Either he hadn't heard her or he didn't care, probably a little of both. But for Abigail, it was a watershed moment of empowerment. She quickly grabbed her cell phone out of her purse and texted Cassie. "I told Nate my name is Abigail and that's what I want to be called."

"What?" came the reply.

"Never mind. I'll explain later."

By the time she started getting ready for bed, Nate wanted to talk further about the meeting. "I thought all the spreadsheets...all my work would, you know, convince Sam I should be next CEO. Good ol' Sammy. He loves your brownies. Dave, too. Ha! Next time put somethin' special in them. Whaddya' think?"

She said nothing and brushed her hair.

"Old Sammy asked Dave for ideas. Dave wasn't ready. But I was. Me. Nate. Plenty ready to be CEO. To take over. Saul acted dumb as usual. Dumb old Saul. Can't do anythin' right."

Nate grabbed Abigail around the waist and pulled her into bed. "What you think? You think old Sammy needs a special brownie? Huh?"

"You're drunk, Nate. Let me go downstairs and get something for you, maybe some PeptoBismol. Your stomach is going to hurt tomorrow."

"Nah. I want me some Abby. Now."

"Not tonight, Nate. You're too drunk. You can't…no…please."

"You're mine. Come on."

"Nate. I said, 'No.'" She tried to get off the bed and slide out from under him, but he outweighed her by at least a hundred pounds.

Finally, it was over. He fell into a stupor, almost immediately snoring. She staggered into the bathroom and sat on the toilet. She screamed into a towel, hating her life, hating the way Nate treated her. She looked around the bathroom for her nightgown, then realized it was still on the bed, ripped into several pieces by her drunken husband. She wrapped her satin robe around her and stumbled down the stairs.

She thought about texting Cassie, but knew her friend would be asleep. Cassie needed her sleep, to stay healthy for the baby. Cassie and her beloved husband, living their perfect life and planning for a wonderful future while she lived with this monster of a man and couldn't see any way out.

What if she called that number Jubilee gave her? But she had thrown the number away in the Sonic trash can. A number for women whose husbands hit them. No numbers for wives whose husbands called them names, treated them like trash and raped them.

Maybe she could call Jubilee. At three thirty in the blessed morning? No. She wasn't even one of Jubilee's regular clients. She couldn't expect a counselor to be available twenty-four seven to a woman who was just a participant in a class.

Maybe call someone at church. Of course not. The pastors were all men, and they wouldn't believe her anyway. Nate was on the deacon board and well-respected. Nobody at the church would believe her.

If she could only run away. But where? How? Nate controlled all the money. She had his credit card he allowed her to use, but he put a limit of $500 on it. That wouldn't get her very far and besides, he could track where she went by the places she used the card. She had seen that happen on CSI one night. An estranged husband found his wife by following the usage on her credit card.

If only her mother still lived. Abigail could go home. Mama would help her. But her mother was dead and dead people can't help anyone.

What about the police? Call 9-1-1 while Nate slept and tell the officers what he did to her. That nice officer

No Visible Scars

Tamara. No. It was a he said, she said problem. The officers couldn't do anything for a domestic dispute, except maybe calm everyone down. They had to actually witness a man hitting his wife or videotape the bruises.

She had no place to go and no options. She could only endure her life with Nate and learn more about boundaries at the next class. If the subject came up, she would ask Jubilee about it, in a roundabout way, without telling everything that happened.

If she were smarter, she would never have married Nate. She would have finished college and found herself a wonderful school where she could teach little children. She would stay single and live her life teaching the offspring of other couples. She would feel safe within her own world. If only.

Maybe Nate was right to call her an abscess. Maybe she *was* a puss-filled sore that constantly re-filled with gook and ugliness. She hated the platinum hair color Nate made her wear. She hated this plastic home they lived in. She hated her job and how she always had to smile and pretend she liked working at the Villas Corporate. She hated fake people who asked, "How are you?" and seemed satisfied when she said, "Fine."

No one knew the ugly truth, and no one cared.

She limped into the kitchen and noticed Nate's dirty dishes on the granite countertop. She started to load them into the dishwasher. Nate hated dirty dishes and wanted her to always keep a clean kitchen. Not tonight, you disgusting and horrible man. Tonight she would leave the dishes on the counter and wash them tomorrow morning, before she and Nate left for work and pretended to be a happy couple.

Four-thirty. It was already tomorrow. No reason to attempt sleep. She would have to be awake by six to make Nate's special breakfast, a protein shake and gluten free muffin. She would prepare his dark roast coffee just as she did every morning. She knew the drill. He would complain of a monster headache and conveniently forget he gave it to himself. He would also forget, or somehow justify, what he had done to her the night before—how he called her 'Abscess,' then proved his warped masculinity by violating her over and over.

Maybe someday she would tell Jubilee all about it. Someday, but not now.

For now, for this moment, she sat on the sofa and waited until the early Kansas sun peeked over the horizon. Another twenty-four hour day to play the role of the devoted wife and meet the needs of everyone except herself.

She texted Cassie and claimed a migraine: "Can't meet for lunch today." Might as well pretend with her friend as well. No need to join Cassie and hear about the wonderful life of her friend.

No, this was a day to hang on to her sanity and find a reason to keep living. She would think about Life Limits Class and all the things Jubilee was teaching them. Somewhere, somehow, maybe she could find a way out of this mess.

CHAPTER TEN

As the class began, Abigail looked around the room and realized how much she enjoyed being with these women. After everyone was seated with their appropriate snacks and drinks, Jubilee asked them to share what they liked best about Life Limits Class.

"Somebody always brings chocolate," Cassie said. "I love chocolate...and pickles...and peanut butter with mayonnaise smeared on Wheat Thins."

"Eew-w," said Ling Su, making a sour face.

Martha massaged her neck and grinned. "Obviously, you've moved past the morning sickness. Enjoy it while you can and eat everything you want. You can lose the baby weight later."

"What about the rest of you?" Jubilee asked. "What have you learned so far about boundaries?"

"It's okay to say, 'No,'" Lydia offered. "I wish I had learned that years ago with my children. They probably wouldn't be mooching off me now if I had been stronger when they were young."

"Sometimes," explained Jubilee, "it's not a matter of strength. Sometimes we just didn't know what tools we possessed or how to use them properly." She scanned the group. "What about you, Abigail? What do you like about our class?"

Abigail picked up the suede taupe pillow and held it close. "I like meeting all of you. I've never really had a group of women I could trust, except for Cassie, of course."

Cassie patted Abigail's hand, then peeled the wrapper off another Hershey's Golden Almond bar.

Abigail grinned and said, "I feel safe here, and you've all given me a sort of foundation to hang on to week after week."

The other women nodded and seemed to agree.

"Being safe is so important," said Jubilee. "What you share is kept in strict confidentiality to ensure safety for your physical and emotional self. But also, we want you to feel you can safely guard your own heart."

"What do you mean?" asked Cassie, licking her fingers and reaching for her water bottle.

Jubilee continued. "Remember the first level of boundaries is our own skin. We should not accept any type of uncomfortable behavior against our skin, whether it's a slap in the face or even someone touching us without invitation. Protect your skin. Set walls of defense around your physical being. You always have the right to say, 'No.'"

Abigail flinched. If skin was the first boundary, she was already behind on setting those life limits.

"Think even deeper," Jubilee said, "beyond your skin. How can you guard your heart? How can you keep your dreams alive and not let anyone destroy them? What are the personal boundaries you need to set?"

"Ooh…I know about this," said Cassie. "I have a dream for my art studio, Smart Art. At first, when Rick and I discussed it, he wasn't too sure. He's a fantastic businessman but everything revolves around the bottom line. So he wanted me to make a certain amount of money and have some security from the get go. But I persisted and reminded him about my creative gifts. I don't want to work as a paralegal forever. Then I met him on his terms and put together a business plan we could work toward. That satisfied him, so I guarded my own heart and kept my dream alive."

"Wonderful example," said Jubilee. "What about the rest of you?"

Amber crossed her arms and frowned at Cassie. "Good for you, but it doesn't always work that way."

"What do you mean?" prodded Jubilee.

"I wanted to travel to France and learn about haute cuisine. Cooking is one of my passions, but I'm stuck in the kitchen with my three kids and end up making mac and cheese or peanut butter sandwiches every night. I told my husband about my hopes of becoming a real chef, maybe I could take a class one night a week at the community college and then save for my trip to France."

Martha sat forward. "Yeah. What'd he say?"

"We had a terrible argument and then we started fighting about lots of other things. Stupid things like who should get up in the middle of the night to change the baby's diaper, who is the real bread winner of the family and stuff like that. We even argued about who should take out the trash. We ended up doing marital counseling with our pastor.

"We told the pastor everything, including my dream about France and how I wanted to use my gifts outside the home." Amber stopped and reached for a Kleenex from the box on the side table. "Lot of good that did me."

Jubilee waited a few moments, then softly said, "Go on. What did your pastor say?"

"He quoted some Bible verses and reminded me that I needed to love, cherish and obey—like what I promised in our wedding vows. He said there might come a day when I could go to France, but in the meantime I needed to support my husband and take care of my children. Something about childcare being a woman's highest calling. My husband, of course, thought that was great advice. We've never talked about my dream since then. It's like a piece of my heart died."

Abigail totally understood how Amber felt. Her dream of becoming a teacher felt withered and dry within her.

Jubilee stood up and paced for a moment. "Ladies, this is one of the reasons I work here. Amber's example is the perfect scenario of spiritual abuse, using one or two passages in the Bible to keep a woman in her place. I would disagree with this pastor, although I respect his position and his role. And certainly, not all pastors would react the same way. Still…the point must be made."

She stood behind her chair and breathed deeply. "Remember ladies, you were designed with gifts and unique personalities before you were even born. That, too, is from a Bible verse. Before the foundation of the world, you were created to do good works. God has given each of you something special to do in life. For some of you, yes, that gifting might include raising a family and supporting your husbands. For others, your gifts might include creativity, leadership or hospitality. Women have abundant possibilities for helping others and making the world a better place. The dream of our hearts has everything to do with what God planted in us before we were born. Usually, the task you love doing is the thing God meant for you to do. You feel you have a purpose, because its significance is so vital to you.

"The most perfect world would be one in which women labor equally alongside men to defeat poverty or to rescue children from sex trafficking or to write and publish great books or any number of incredible tasks. We need to work together and not degrade each other just because one gender is different from the other."

"Wow!" said Cassie.

"Preach it, sister," said Martha.

Jubilee sat back down. "Okay. I'm finished telling you what I think. Let's talk about our assignment for last week. Did any of you have a breakthrough? Did you set a new boundary?"

Ling Su, who usually remained silent during class and wrote careful notes on a yellow legal pad, sat up straight and said, "I need to now say something. This boundaries subject I have thought much of, and believe I try now to make a rule, a boundary, in my heart. This week, I take assignment and walk to Plaza in Kansas City. I leave work at home and do one hour of enjoyment. I sit outside and watch people pass by and think about my country and how we work so hard but often do not play. This week, I played one hour."

Everyone clapped. Ling Su bowed her head and doodled a blue circle on her legal pad.

"Thank you for sharing." Jubilee smiled broadly. "You have indeed guarded your heart this week and set a new boundary for yourself. I am so proud of you. We all are."

"Well...I'll be next," said Lydia. "I had a meeting with my kids and told them we would have to make some changes. From now on, my son is going to have to do his own wash. He's twenty-two years old, for cryin' out loud. He can throw his own dirty socks in the washer and add a bit of soap. Then I told my daughter she could make the family dinner two nights a week and give me a break. After all, I'm the one who's working two jobs. My husband works hard, too. These grown kids can do something."

"Good for you, Lydia. That is outstanding," Jubilee said.

"Well, at least it's a start. Of course, both of my kids griped about it, but my son actually did a load of wash. I think he got tired of smelling his own filthy socks, and I wasn't about to pick 'em up anymore."

"Excellent! Anybody else?"

Abigail wanted to share her own boundary-setting. These women had been vulnerable and honest. She could do the same. It was safe here. She cleared her throat. "It was a tiny step for me, but at least I did it."

"Go on," urged Jubilee, as Abigail stopped and looked at Cassie, trying to gain courage from her friend.

"I don't like it when my husband calls me nicknames. I like my name, Abigail. And that's what I want to be called.

But I guess I've never really told him that, so maybe he didn't know. Maybe it's my fault."

"Stop right there," said Jubilee. "Nobody is placing any blame on anyone. We're just working toward our goals. Okay, Abigail. What did you do? How did you set a boundary?"

"I told him my name is Abigail and that's what I want to be called. Not Abby. Not anything else. Just Abigail."

She didn't tell the ladies how Nate continued to call her Abscess or Abby whenever he chose. But setting her small boundary felt like one step forward.

"We're proud of you," said Jubilee, "and you have our permission, in case we slip up and call you Abby. Just remind us you are Abigail." Jubilee took a sip of her water. "It's important to know the history of our names, to remind us how unique we are. To give us a clue about who God created us to be and what we can someday become."

Jubilee pulled a leather-bound book off the bookshelf. "This is a book of names. All of you can look up your names after class, if you'd like." She licked her finger and turned several pages toward the front of the book. "Ah, here it is. 'Abigail, source of joy.'" Jubilee closed the book and handed it to Lydia.

Abigail shook her head. "I don't feel much like a source of joy. I'm not sure about that definition."

"I get it," said Cassie. "You make me feel joyful because you're my friend. And when I do fun things with you or drive you here to Life Limits Class, that makes me feel joyful. You *are* a source of joy."

"But you're my friend. You would feel that way if my name was…I don't know…Bertha or something."

"Nah, I get it, too," said Martha, adjusting her pillow behind her back. "In fact, while we're talking about it, I just want to say congrats to you, kiddo. You told your hubby what's what and the name you want to be called. In my book, that took a lot of guts, so you gave me some joy tonight."

"Absolutely," said Jubilee. "You give me great joy, Abigail, every time you walk into this room, because I know how important boundary-setting is to you. You bring me joy each week, by allowing me to share the importance of life limits with you."

Kathy laid her notebook upside down on her lap. "My turn. I've seen a great deal of growth in you, Abigail. Each week, it seems you listen intently to everything that is shared. I can almost see the wheels spinning in your head." She smiled and pushed her glasses up higher on her nose. "I think what you've shared tonight is incredible. For me as well, you bring a source of great joy, knowing how much you've grown in this area of setting life limits."

Abigail felt her face flush. "Thank you," she said softly. Cassie reached an arm around her and hugged her close.

"I'd like to know," continued Kathy, "what is the desire of your heart, Abigail? Is there a dream hidden somewhere in you, something special you want to do?"

If she spoke it, maybe it would come true. These women had been honest with her. They waited patiently for her answer.

"Okay," she said. "Yes, I do have a dream, but I don't know if it can happen. Maybe...all of you can help me grow stronger until someday, it becomes a reality."

The women leaned forward, their eagerness to help her a physical symbol of drawing her out, urging her as one unit to speak the secret of her soul.

"A teacher," said Abigail, and almost immediately, tears welled up in her throat. "I want to be a teacher so badly...to show little children how to read and write, how to count and how to treat each other with respect. That's what I want. That's the dream of my heart."

Cassie reached for a Kleenex and pulled several from the box. She dabbed at her own face, then handed a couple of clean ones to Abigail who swallowed her tears and started to shred the tissues. Tiny pieces of white salted her beige slacks.

"And another thing," said Abigail. "Another thing I want so badly. Oh, it's probably silly."

"Nothing is silly," said Jubilee, "when it reflects what is in our hearts."

"Okay then. Here it is. I hate these slacks. I hate my clothes. I hate that my husband makes me wear taupe and beige and white and black and everything ugly because it makes me feel ugly. I'm so tired of these stupid clothes. I wish I could tear them up and throw them away and never, ever wear them again."

The release of truth gushed out. She rammed her fist onto her lips, afraid she might tell everything about her life with Nate.

"Thank you," said Jubilee, "for sharing your truth." She looked around the room and seemed to focus on every woman. "You know, if we don't share our truth, if we don't use our voices, then we remain invisible and nothing changes."

Remain invisible. Abigail wondered if she would ever become her true self. What did that even look like?

"Just a minute," said Jubilee. "I have an idea." She hurried into an adjoining room, then returned to the group and walked toward Abigail, holding something behind her back.

"Every time you come to Life Limits Class, I will have this on the table for you to wear." She reached out and wound a beautiful gold and purple scarf around Abigail's neck. "You can wear it for the duration of the class and test how it feels next to your skin. It's definitely not taupe or beige, and you have my permission to wear it as long as you like. In fact, I am giving it to you, to remind you that you are definitely *not* ugly. You *are* a source of joy. Come over here with me."

Abigail stood and followed Jubilee to the mirror which hung in the corner. She looked at herself, at the fake hair color she hated and the worry lines between her dark eyebrows. The gold and purple scarf shimmered around her neck, giving off a glow of beauty. The beginnings of a smile teased Abigail's face and one dimple winked.

Jubilee put her arm around Abigail's waist. "Don't ignore the dream inside you. Sometimes we women ignore our dreams, then blame our misery on God. The truth is...he wants us to have the desires of our hearts, to develop those dreams he placed within us before we ever saw our mother's face. Have the courage to live your dream. I know you can do it."

Suddenly, the rest of the women appeared in the mirror's reflection. The bluish-gray hair of Lydia next to the almond-shaped eyes of Ling Su. Cassie, with her shiny highlights and her eyes still moist from empathy tears. Martha, Amber and Missy behind Abigail while Kathy stood respectfully on the other side of Jubilee. The faces, a continuum of harmony, women who shared a sisterhood with their flaws and their learning curves, guided by this one woman with her warm smile and her white hair, that rebellious black streak down the side.

Jubilee addressed them all. "We must join together to help each other be better yet not lose ourselves in the process, to never be satisfied with a victim mentality but use our strengths to march forward with passion and courage. Follow your heart's cry into a new version of authenticity. Be yourselves and learn to love yourselves, because you cannot truly love others or even receive love until you begin to respect yourselves. Set your boundaries, then find the freedom to open your hearts and live your dreams."

They gathered even closer together, a cadre of warriors with their arms around Abigail. As they rocked together, they chanted like a sports team, cheering her on, "Ab-i-gail, Ab-i-gail, Ab-i-gail."

Tears streamed down her cheeks as she felt the love that permeated from these women, these companions who were learning more about themselves and the protective walls they could place around their hearts.

Abigail looked at Cassie's reflection in the mirror. Then she caught Jubilee's eye and grinned.

"Source of joy," said Jubilee. "Always remember that, Abigail. You *are* a source of joy."

CHAPTER ELEVEN

As Abigail quietly let herself into the front door that night, she felt an inner glow of happiness. Love and acceptance from the women of the Life Limits class wrapped around her like a warm blanket. She still wore her beige clothing, but she knew the beautiful gold and purple scarf was hers to wear each Wednesday. She wanted to soak in the memory of this night and how it felt to be surrounded by all those women who thought she was beautiful, gifted and a source of joy.

But when she hung her purse on the hall tree, a shiver of apprehension interrupted her joy. Nate. In the glow of what had happened, she had almost forgotten she had to be her drab old self again and face her husband.

"So…what did you study tonight, Abby? At your little Bible study?" He stood in the doorway that led to the kitchen, a drumstick in his hand. He took a bite and waited.

"Oh, uhm, let's see…what was that passage? First John three, I think. Yeah. That was it. First John three."

"Really? And what was the main topic in that passage?"

Drat! She and Cassie had been so thrilled about what happened during Life Limits Class, they hadn't rehearsed what she should tell Nate. They always decided together, before she went into the house, just in case he grilled her on the evening's activities. But not tonight. Tonight, they forgot.

"I'm waiting." He took another bite of the drumstick.

Maybe if she changed the subject. "Would you like me to fix you some mashed potatoes to go with that chicken? I forgot to leave any side dishes tonight. Would you like that?"

"I don't want any freakin' potatoes, Abby. I want you to answer my question. What did you study tonight?"

"Oh, Nate, why does it matter? I'm really tired. Can't we just go to bed? I'll massage your feet, if you like." She moved past him into the kitchen and opened the fridge. She reached for a carton of yogurt, then opened the drawer to find a spoon. He was suddenly beside her.

"Guess what I did tonight, little Abscess? Just guess."

"I don't know, and please don't call me that name. Did you work late?"

His breath didn't smell like alcohol, and another shiver of fear ran up her spine. Sometimes the alcohol slightly sedated him, but tonight he seemed completely sober, frighteningly alert.

"I made a phone call," he said. "To Cassie's church, to her pastor. I Googled his name and contact info. Did you forget I could do that, sweet Abby?"

"What? Cassie's pastor?"

"That's right. I called Pastor Jim and guess what? He doesn't know anything about a women's Bible study on Wednesday nights. He checked the church schedule, and of course, if there *was* a Bible study, his wife would be involved. But she isn't at the Bible study, and do you know why? Because there *is* no Bible study on Wednesday nights at Cassie's church."

Nate dropped the drumstick on the counter, his brows knit together in a scowl."Then I called Cassie's husband and guess what that dope said? He didn't know where you girls were. He doesn't keep tabs on his wife. Imagine that! Doesn't even know where his wife is on a week night."

He moved closer, pounded his right fist into his left palm. "Where the hell have you been going every week? Is Cassie dropping you off somewhere to meet another man? Are you doing one of those depraved things where women go to a bar and watch naked men dance? What are you two lame-brained girls doing? Huh? I want to know right now. Tell me the truth."

Nate snatched the yogurt carton out of Abigail's hand and hurled it onto the patio's French doors. The carton split open. Peach mango oozed down the window pane.

Abigail backed up to the granite counter top. Her heart raced as she silently prayed, *Help me, help me, please.*

Nate grabbed her wrist and twisted it until the pain reached all the way to her shoulder. "Where were you tonight? Tell me…now." He dropped her wrist and moved in closer, trapping her from any escape.

A whiff of greasy chicken. "I really don't want to tell you. Don't make me…uhm…spoil the surprise."

"Surprise? What are you talking about? What's going on?"

She rubbed her wrist, tried to make the pain ease. "Okay, but remember. You made me tell." She cleared her throat, willing her brain to work, to think of something. "Cassie and I have been taking a class."

"A class? What kind of class?"

"It's a...a crafts class. We're taking a crafts class."

"What? Like knitting or something? You don't knit."

"There are other crafts besides knitting, and we wanted it to be a secret."

"Why? What's the big deal?" Nate backed up a bit.

Abigail took a deep breath. "We're doing crafts so we can make a special gift for you and Rick. It's a class with other wives who want to make something personal for their husbands. Now please...don't ask me anything else, because I don't want to spoil the surprise."

She grabbed a roll of paper towels and moved toward the French doors. Her heart slowly stopped thumping. She glanced back at Nate who stood by the counter, a slight grin on his face.

"Humph. A gift for the husbands? Well...thanks." He ran his hand through his hair. "Hey, I shouldn't have done that, you know, grabbed you like that. I don't know why...uhm...I don't know." He crossed the kitchen and moved closer. "What can I do to make it up to you? You want to go out for some ice cream or a pizza maybe?"

She rubbed off the last of the yogurt and turned around to face him. "No. I don't want to go anywhere, but there *is* something you can do to make up."

"Yeah, what?" A sly grin crossed his face. He reached out a finger to stroke her cheek.

No Visible Scars

Abigail shivered. "No. Not that. I don't want sex. What you can do, Nate, is call me by my real name."

"What?"

"That's right. You can call me Abigail. Not Abby and certainly not Abscess. Call me by my real name."

"Well...okay. I don't know why it's such a big deal, but I'll try to remember that."

"Thank you. Now go on up to bed, and I'll be there in a minute. After I finish cleaning up this mess."

He turned toward the stairs. Then almost as an afterthought, faced her again. "Forgot to tell you. I was packing when you came home and then got sort of distracted."

"Packing?"

"Yeah. I'm leaving tomorrow for the Villa in Peoria. I'll be there through the weekend and fly back on Sunday night. Sam wants me to take a more proactive approach, visit each of the branches at least every two weeks. Make sure the staff are happy and new residents filling up the empty spaces. I'll leave tomorrow morning about six. You can drive me to the airport."

Stunned, she didn't know how to respond. She knew Samuel and the board were making changes, but she had no idea how those changes might affect her life. Every two weeks Nate would be gone for a few days? What kind of wonderful gift was this?

"Okay. The airport at six. You'd better get to sleep. I'll be upstairs in a minute."

No Visible Scars

She watched as he climbed the stairs. Then waited until she heard him go into the bathroom and turn on the water to brush his teeth and gargle three times. His regular routine.

Clutching the roll of paper towels to her chest, she twirled around the kitchen. Glory, hallelujah! Freedom every two weeks. A few wonderful days without worrying about how to please Nate, how to avoid his anger, how to live as *he* wanted her to live.

She twirled again. She had done it. She had made it clear to Nate that she wanted to be called Abigail. This time he heard her. This time he understood. Maybe he would follow through. Maybe not. But at least, she was proud of herself for taking this step.

She wanted to tell Cassie and Jubilee, but not now. She cleaned the wood on the French doors and whispered a prayer. "God, I'm sorry I lied to my husband tonight, but I had to make up that story about the crafts class. It was the only thing I could say that wouldn't make him angrier. Surely you understand."

No answer in return. She looked upward at the ceiling, "I don't know if you will forgive me, but thank you anyway. Tomorrow night, Nate will be in Peoria. I'm sorry for whatever I've done wrong in my whole life. But thank you for this gift of freedom."

In the bathroom, Abigail cleaned off her makeup in slow motion and smiled at her reflection. Source of joy. Tonight, she would revel in that joy and hopefully sleep in peace. When the alarm sounded in the morning, she would drive Nate to the airport and then do something to celebrate.

Maybe take Cassie out for coffee. Maybe take a longer lunch than usual. Maybe ask David for the afternoon off and stroll through the Plaza, alone. She had never shopped in the Plaza, or anywhere else for that matter, without Nate beside her, holding her elbow and leading her into the stores he liked, choosing the clothes he wanted her to wear.

It was almost too much to imagine. She would call Jubilee and tell her the good news. In the morning. Tomorrow.

No Visible Scars

CHAPTER TWELVE

"You did what?" Cassie sipped her Orange Julius and crunched into a dill pickle.

Abigail speared a bite of arugula salad. "Okay. I know a crafts class was a stretch, but I couldn't tell him the truth about Life Limits Class. He would never let me go. I'd be trapped in the house every Wednesday night."

Cassie smiled. "Actually, it was quite brilliant, to feed on his ego that you were making him a special gift. So what shall *we* make for dear old Nate? Any ideas?"

"None. You're the artist. I figure you'll come up with something wonderful once our class ends. You know…I'm really going to miss that bunch of ladies. And Jubilee. She's the best."

"Uh-huh. It's been a great group. Maybe we can convince Jubilee to extend the class, give us time to learn more."

"That would be great." Abigail finished playing around with the leftovers of her salad and pushed the bowl away.

Cassie reached for it. "You're not going to eat those radish curls? Really, girl. That's the best part."

"You go for it while I sit here, watch you eat and enjoy my freedom. I can't believe I have the whole day, an entire Friday to play. David was wonderful to give me this day off and how lucky you had the same day free. I feel like a kid playing hooky, and Nate won't be back home for two days. Heavenly!" Abigail leaned back and breathed in the summer air. "So…what are we going to do?"

"We're going shopping, silly. What else? And…I have a great idea of something special for you."

"For me? No, we should find something crafty for the guys, something Nate thinks I could actually make for him, something he and Rick would both enjoy."

"Now that I think of it, I have a couple of things in my stash that I'm saving for the new store. I made them years ago when I was playing with mosaics. I broke a couple of dishes to make colorful pieces, then pasted them together with plaster of Paris into a design. They turned out to be these cool coasters. You can give one of them to Nate. Easy peasy."

"Perfect. He likes anything he can use at work. He'll have something to set his 'I'm Number One' coffee cup on. So maybe we can shop for the baby. Do you know yet? Boy or girl?"

"We've decided we want it to be a surprise. I already have lots of baby stuff. No girlfriend, today we're shopping for you. Let's go. Lunch is on me." Cassie finished filling out the ticket the waitress had given her, signed her name with a flourish and used her arms to raise herself out of her chair.

No Visible Scars

Abigail grabbed Cassie's elbow to help her up. "Are you sure you're not having twins?"

"No chance. The doctor said it's a big baby, and I can't stop eating. So this kid must have a heck of an appetite." Cassie moved sideways around several tables. "You're driving, right?"

"Sure." As soon as they were both buckled in, Abigail carefully steered her Acura through the streets of Westport and onto I-35. She and Cassie both liked the stores in Park Place but a new Von Maur had opened on Metcalf. Abigail started in that direction, but Cassie said, "Ooh, Penney's. We have to go there first."

"Why? What's at Penney's?"

"The salon. We're both getting a trim, and I have a new color idea for you."

"For me? You know Nate likes this platinum blonde #23. I hate it, but there's no changing his mind."

"Just follow my lead, girl. I have a plan."

She wanted to hug Cassie, but she was too busy searching for a parking spot that wouldn't be too far to walk. Then she spotted a place next to the handicapped sign that was tagged "For Expectant Mothers."

"Here we go," Abigail said as she pulled in and turned off the ignition.

Inside the salon, Cassie chatted with one of the hair stylists who had obviously been expecting them. "Yeah," Cassie explained, "I made this appointment yesterday when we started planning our fun day. George here is great. He's gonna' fix you up while Sally works on me."

113

No Visible Scars

George chatted about his new apartment while he massaged Abigail's neck. It made her feel uncomfortable to have a man touch her, but since Cassie had arranged this appointment, she hated to throw a wrench into this fun day.

"Now my darling, what shall we do with this mass of hair you have? How about a new style, something a bit more modern? Yes?"

"Uh, no. My husband likes my hair as it is. Just a little trim, please, and a shampoo and style."

"But my darling," George said as he frowned and worked his fingers into Abigail's scalp. "This color is all wrong for you. With your beautiful amber eyes, I see you in auburn with a touch of gold. How about that? Let me strip this ugly color away and give you some beautiful gold and auburn highlights. Yes?"

"Again, no. Actually, I was born with auburn hair, but my husband...."

"Oh, yes, the husband. Why must my clients always be with the husband who has no style? I ask myself this. All right, my darling. We will trim this platinum mess and then shampoo you, but all this against my better judgment."

"Thank you, George."

While Abigail waited for her hair to condition under the soft white towel George wrapped around her head, Cassie whispered something to George.

"But of course," he said. "This is the perfect solution. Madame, you are a genius. I know just the style, and I will look in our selection to find the perfect one. You have made me happy this day."

No Visible Scars

Abigail closed her eyes and tried to enjoy the pampering. Cassie had even arranged for manis and pedis at the same salon. An hour later, they sat in adjoining chairs while two petite girls scrubbed the balls of their feet with pumice stones. Abigail giggled and flinched as the stone hit her tickle spot. It felt so wonderful to be cared for, to know that Nate was far away in Peoria and all she had to do was seize the day.

"Turquoise," said Cassie. "I want turquoise with a little white flower on the big toes and my thumbs. And for my friend, how about deep purple with a yellow flower?"

"Oh, no. I can't. Nate would never allow it." Abigail pulled her hands back and shook her head.

"But Nate isn't here right now and this is just for us. Come on. Try something different."

She tried to roll the tenseness out of her shoulders. But Cassie was right. Nate would be gone for another two days. Live a little. "All right. Glossy purple, but just for a few days. I'll have to take it off before Nate comes home."

"Let's think of it as pushing the boundaries a little."

As her nails dried, they looked and felt wonderful. But she was completely surprised when George reappeared. "And now you come with me again, please," he said.

"But I thought we were finished, George. You did a great job on my hair. Thanks." She caught a glance of herself in the mirror. Her hair hung halfway down her back in a soft avalanche of waves.

Cassie giggled and followed Abigail back to George's station where he uncovered a wig head. "Ta-da," he announced with a flourish.

"What?" Abigail looked at the wig, a blunt cut with a rich auburn color and a few select highlights around the face. "Surprise!" said Cassie. "Try it on."

George quickly gathered Abigail's hair into a bun at the top of her head, clipped it securely, then snugly fit on the wig. The transformation was amazing. "Did I not tell you," he said, as he twirled Abigail around so she could see herself in the mirror. "This is your color, my darling. You must wear this always. Let George strip that nasty platinum away from you forever."

"Wow!" said Cassie. "You are so beautiful."

Abigail slowly raised her eyes to the mirror and then sucked in a quick breath. This was the face she remembered from her first year of college, before Nate made her change. This was her true self. A bit shorter style than she was used to, but the auburn wig brought out the color of her skin and seemed to light a glow in her eyes.

"Cassie...I don't know what to say...George...." she stuttered, afraid to admit how much she liked the new look because she would have to give it up.

"We'll take it," said Cassie. "My gift to you for your birthday."

"My birthday isn't until October, and where can I...when can I wear this?"

They both exclaimed at the same time, "Life Limits Class."

George looked puzzled.

"Never mind," said Cassie as she handed him a tip. "Thanks for all your help."

No Visible Scars

As Cassie paid for their services at the checkout, George waved at Abigail. "You remember now. When you are ready to be transformed permanently, you march right back to George."

Cassie and Abigail waltzed out of the salon, their arms around each other. Cassie's turquoise toes sparkled as they walked outside, and Abigail could barely keep herself from looking in every mirror, every window and every reflection. She absolutely loved the color on her toes and fingernails and every time she saw herself with the auburn wig, she smiled all over again.

"Now to Von Maur," said Cassie.

"I don't know if I can stand anymore kindness today. Thank you so much."

"Oh, nonsense. We haven't even started with the biggest surprise. Come on, let's see what we can find. I'm dying to see this new store."

They shopped for a half hour and found a comfortable maternity tee shirt, teal blue with the words "Baby Mama" in sparkles on the front. Cassie paid for her purchase, then grabbed the sack and said, "Now...on to the dresses."

"You're getting a dress, too?"

"No, silly. This one is for you."

"What? I don't need a dress. Nate makes me wear slacks or pencil skirts at work, and at home, I wear sweats."

"Forget about Nate and what he likes. Today, we're shopping for you. OMG, every time I look at you in that wig, I get goose bumps. You're stunning, girl."

Abigail giggled and let Cassie lead her to the dresses section. So many choices, and she was so accustomed to black and beige. Although the clothes were obviously top of the line, she couldn't make a decision. Nate would never allow her to wear any of these satiny wonders, bright colors or prints.

What in the world was the matter? She used to love shopping—years ago—before Nate. Now she felt numb, as if she could no longer think for herself.

It was Cassie who found it. A slinky matte jersey fabric with a ruche waistline and draped bodice. But it was the color that made Abigail gasp. A floral print of brilliant blues with solid satin buttons at the shoulders. It was sleeveless and hit just above Abigail's knees when she tried it on. She pirouetted in front of the triple mirrors in the dressing room while Cassie applauded.

"Unbelievable! You're like a monarch butterfly who just came out of her cocoon. I've got to take a picture. Hold still." Cassie aimed her cell phone and took several shots, directing Abigail as if she was on a movie set. "Now let's have a side view. Perfect. How about a head shot? Come on now, a big smile for the Baby Mama."

"But Cassie, this is ridiculous. It's amazingly beautiful, and I love it. It feels so…I don't know…luxurious and silky. It makes me feel like a completely different person."

"You know what that color of blue stands for, don't ya'? Bright royal blue is a symbol of freedom, of strength. It stands for new beginnings. Pretty optimistic, right?"

No Visible Scars

"Freedom and strength." Abigail sighed. "But where will I wear it? Of course, one time to Life Limits Class but then what? And I can't keep it in my closet. Nate would be furious."

"Easy peasy! We keep your dress and your wig at my house. Then when you have your weekends away from Nate, we dress up and go out on the town. Simple!"

She thought for a moment. "That will work for a while, but at some point, I'll need to set some limits with Nate and wear what I want. Practice those important boundaries. Okay. You keep the dress and the wig for now. I'll let you know when I'm ready for freedom and strength."

She felt all warm inside, cared for and loved until she looked at the price tag. She carefully slipped the dress over her head and put on her beige blouse. "No way. Nate would have a fit. $118.99? Are you kidding? He never allows me to spend over fifty dollars at one time without his pre-approval. He'll blow a gasket when he sees this bill. How will I ever explain it?"

Cassie carried the dress on its hangar out of the dressing room. "You're not talking to a dummy here," she said. "This dress is already paid for."

"No." She grabbed Cassie's arm. "I can't let you do this. You've already paid for the salon, for the wig, for lunch. No more. I can't ever pay you back."

Cassie sighed. "This was supposed to be a secret, but since you're being a butthead about it...." She kissed Abigail on the cheek. "Remember that night at Life Limits class when Jubilee told you about the meaning of your name and you said you hated your clothes?"

"Sure. Yes."

"Well, when you went to the bathroom to fix your face, we all took up a little love offering."

"What?"

"That's right, girlfriend. It was Martha's idea and everybody pitched in. We have just enough to buy this dress and a little extra for the tax and a treat. So there! Done and done."

Abigail stumbled to a chair outside the dressing room, plopped down and let the tears flow. These women had gifted her with so much. First, they had surrounded her in class and helped her feel valued, then they believed in the desire of her heart and decided to make it a reality. She didn't deserve this. She couldn't accept it.

"Aw, honey," Cassie put her arms around Abigail and hugged her tight. "Just enjoy the moment. Come on. I said we had enough left over for a treat. There's a Ben and Jerry's across Metcalf. Let's go have a scoop of something wonderful."

CHAPTER THIRTEEN

Before she picked up Nate at the airport, Abigail rubbed off the purple nail polish. It took several applications of polish remover. Gone were her rich-looking, wonderfully gratifying nails. A pile of cotton balls, tinged with the color of hope, lay near the bathroom sink. She quickly swept them into a plastic bag, tied it three times with tight knots and ran outside to toss it in the dumpster.

Back inside, she brushed through her hair, hating the color even more, now that she knew how she looked in a different color and style. But the next time Nate left, she and Cassie would play dress up. She could once again be her true self, wear her freedom and strength with the wig and the royal blue dress.

A sliver of disappointment shadowed her soul. She could never be her authentic self if she kept pretending to be who Nate wanted her to be. With Cassie, she could behave freely, breathe again. But it was a different story at home. Somehow she had to merge the two halves of her life together.

Nate slid into the front seat. "The time in Peoria went great, but we've got to do a better job of public relations, starting right here in the Metro. Take some of your brownies to the Villas in Overland Park. Give them to the staff and visit some of the residents. Build up the PR. Dave and I will do more engagement in some of the other branches. When the staff and residents see how much the corporate office cares, maybe we'll get extra referrals. It's called asset marketing."

It sounded like a good plan. That night she stirred up a new batch of brownies in her favorite Cambria bowl. She thought about Mama and the joy they shared each time they baked together. They sampled the dough, added the secret ingredient, then shared a warm brownie sometimes topped with a scoop of vanilla ice cream. She inserted a CD of cheerful Josh Groban music to distract herself, afraid she might cry all over the cocoa powder. How she missed Mama! How different her life would be if Mama was still alive. She would tell Mama how life with Nate had soured.

She bit into a fresh brownie, ran her tongue around the chocolate chips and swiped at a tear. Comfort food could not solve everything. After the brownies cooled, she packed them into a Tupperware container and placed them in the freezer.

At work the next day, she called the director at the Overland Park Villa and made an appointment for Thursday. "I made a batch of brownies last night," she told the director. "I'll bring them for your staff."

"Excellent. We always love treats in the break room."

As she scanned through current emails, she noticed one from Cassie. The subject line read "One Hot Lady." She clicked open the email and saw the picture of herself wearing the beautiful blue dress and the auburn wig. She gasped, then

No Visible Scars

moved her curser over the picture to delete it, in case Nate passed by. But something stopped her.

She stared at her reflection, smiling with confidence, wrapped in the ruched waistline and glowing from Cassie's approval. A beautiful image in royal blue covering the drab executive assistant. She took a deep breath, then printed out the picture before she deleted the email.

Now to hide it. To remind herself of who she could be, the real Abigail who lived somewhere within. Use it as a token of personal encouragement on days when she felt hopeless. But if Nate ever saw that picture…. He would tear it into tiny pieces and throw it right at her. Or worse.

She pulled out a sheet of paper from the printer and made a little pouch, taping the sides together. Then she folded the picture and slipped it into the pouch. A couple of strips of tape secured the pouch on the underside of her top desk drawer. Nate would never see it, but she could pull it out occasionally and look at it. Dream about wearing the luxurious dress and doing something different with her hair. Reflect on who she really was, her true authenticity.

She grinned just as Nate walked out of his office and marched toward her, his steps quick and determined. "What are you smiling about?"

"Nothing. I just made an appointment to visit one of the Villas like you told me to. What's wrong with smiling at work?"

His right eyebrow raised. "There's nothing wrong with smiling as long as you have a good reason. We have a lot to do today, and I don't want you goofing off."

David rounded the corner. "I've never seen Abigail goof off. Lighten up, Nate." David strolled toward the fax machine and inserted a page, then punched several buttons.

Nate scowled. "'Lighten up,' he says. When we're under the gun to finish another marketing project for Sam and the board. Lighten up. Sure! How's that gonna' happen?"

"Oh, I don't know," said David. "How about tonight we all go to a special place I know for some drinks and soft music? I'll ask Michele and we can make it a foursome."

Abigail wanted to say, "Sure," but she knew before he spoke what Nate's response would be.

"We can't afford to be romping around town when we have a business to run. Besides, I don't like your kind of music. All that poetic stuff and twelve-string guitars."

"Suit yourself. Abigail, you want to go with Michele and me?"

Oh, to have the freedom to wear her new dress and go to a fun place, listen to soft music and sway to the beat of lyrical sound. What a joy that would be! But she knew what her response needed to be. No sense making Nate more tense. His pointer finger tapped against her computer monitor.

An inward sigh. "Thanks, David, but I'll stay here and help Nate with whatever he needs. I hope you and Michele have a wonderful time."

"We will. In fact, I'm trying out one of my new songs tonight. Wanta' hear it? I have my guitar in the office."

"No," said Nate. "Abby and I don't want to hear your latest song, especially not here in the office. And I wish

No Visible Scars

you'd stop bringing your guitar to work. I can't concentrate when you're strumming that thing and caterwauling down the hallway. Knock it off, Dave."

Abigail dug her nails into her palms. Abby again. When would Nate ever learn?

David picked up his paper from the fax machine, then waved it in Nate's face. "Writing poems and putting them to music is how I work best, and you don't own my corner of the office. So get off my case. I know how to work the business as well as you. I just have different methods. Besides, I was here until midnight last night, and I pulled an all-nighter last week." David opened the door to the outside hallway. "I'm going out for a Coke, to that little deli down the street, to clear my head. I'll be back in an hour or so. Abigail, please take any messages for me."

"Certainly," she said.

Nate hurried into his office and slammed the door. She tried to think of something to soothe him, but she knew it would take him a while to cool down. It took all her self-restraint not to close up the office and leave, to follow David to that little deli and ask him to sing his latest song. But Nate would want her to stay in the office and support him, no matter what. Point and click. Point and click.

Make a special meal tonight or promise to rub his shoulders, anything to keep him calm. Maybe some chicken tetrazzini and a Caesar salad. A big glass of Merlot, of course.

She carefully pulled out her top drawer and reached inside the hidden pouch to feel the picture. If only she could figure out a way to escape, to go with David and Michele for a night on the town, to experience such lovely freedom.

No use wishing for something she could not have. She closed her drawer and maneuvered her mouse over another Excel chart. Point and click. Point and click.

❧❧❧

On Thursday, she packed up her brownies and drove to the Villa de Comfort in Overland Park. She always felt a sense of pride when she visited any of the Villas. Every location exuded comfort as well as the finest quality of care and design, each Villa with its own flair. This one sported the more traditional, Southern plantation design. Large pillars supported the front porch entwined in Spanish moss and other vines. A few morning glories peeked out between the greenery while several garden benches and patio chairs offered comfortable seating around the perimeter of the porch.

Abigail paused for a moment and stroked a petal from one of the morning glories. A droplet of dew clung to her forefinger. She rubbed it with her thumb. Oh to spend moments of leisure in one of these chairs, to forget about the corporate hassle and revel in these droplets of dew, those patches of sunlight winking through the vines.

Inside, she marveled at the tapestry rug that ran up the spiral staircase. She knew the healthier residents lived upstairs, those who still climbed stairs or could identify the correct buttons on the massive elevator that now dinged as it landed on the first floor. The wing to the right led to assisted living while the left corridor remained closed behind a coded door, reserved for those residents who lived in Memory Care, locked within an Alzheimer's diagnosis.

She headed toward the director's office, marked by bronze placards down the hallway. A woman at a massive desk sat with a phone receiver next to her ear. She motioned Abigail to the floral wing chair in the corner and mouthed "Just a minute."

With her Tupperware container on her lap, she sat unobtrusively. She noticed a certificate of achievement for the Villas de Comfort of Overland Park, Kansas—awarded one of the finest institutions in the Kansas City Metro. On one level, she felt proud of the work they accomplished, to provide a beautiful living space for these elderly men and women. On another level, she longed to disappear into a younger world and teach little ones their A-B-C's.

The director hung up the phone. "I'm so sorry," she said. "This has been one of those days. I assume you're Abigail from the corporate office?"

"Yes, and I've brought the brownies, as I promised." She opened the container lid and passed it to the director who grabbed one and immediately gobbled a massive bite.

"Oh, my word, these are amazing. You have saved my life. I was so hungry for chocolate. Delicious!" She finished off the last of that brownie and grabbed a second. With her mouth full, she managed to mumble, "Sorry. My name is Melissa. Let me show you around."

She scooted out from her desk and motioned for Abigail to precede her through the doorway and into the hallway. "I assume you've never been here?" she asked as she reached for yet another brownie.

"Not to this particular Villa," said Abigail as she closed the Tupperware container. "But I know the important work you all do here."

"Yes," said Melissa. "We work hard to make this the most comfy place in the city for our residents, and of course to assure families their loved ones are well taken care of. Here's the staff break room. You can leave the brownies here, if you'd like. I'm sure they'll be gobbled up in no time. How about a copy of the recipe?"

"No. I can't do that. I've kept it a secret all these years, ever since my mother and I baked together. I will, however, be glad to bring another batch some time."

"Wonderful! Let me know when you're coming and I'll diet for three days before I make a pig of myself again." Melissa showed Abigail the expansive dining room, already set for the next meal with yellow linen tablecloths and coordinating napkins of a striped yellow and blue print. A waiter pushed through the adjoining kitchen door. The aroma of baking chicken filled the area.

"This is beautiful," said Abigail. "Appetizing and cozy at the same time."

"And our chef is one of the best in Kansas City. None of our residents starve, I can assure you. In fact, meal time is one of the highlights of each day."

They peeked inside the hair salon. Abigail's nose tickled from the pungent smell of a perm. She sneezed. They quickly moved to the craft room, lined with shelves filled with markers, beads, paint brushes and small frames. Several easels stood around the room, portraying still life's, landscapes and self-portraits.

A beeper on Melissa's waistband sounded. "I apologize," she said, "but I need to get back to my office. Make yourself at home and don't forget to visit Room 103, the corner suite, one of our special residents. You'll find her suite down this hallway. 'Bye now." Melissa hurried off, leaving Abigail to wander alone.

She returned to the staff break room and wrapped a couple of brownies inside a napkin, then placed them in her purse. Might as well have something delicious to share when she met the resident of Room 103, to break the awkwardness of a first meeting.

As she walked down the hallway Melissa had indicated, she heard television sets on high volume blasting the news or an occasional weather report. Each apartment with its own type of decoration beside the doorway: a planter with a trailing philodendron vine, a teddy bear dressed in a Kansas City Royals T-shirt, a collection of gardening utensils still shiny and obviously unused.

Outside Room 103, Abigail paused and read the bronze placard posted on the doorframe: Ruth Judah. A bronze vase with yellow roses hung on the door. She knocked timidly two times, then wondered if this Ruth person might have a hearing problem. She rapped harder three more times.

"Please come in," answered a pleasant voice.

She turned the doorknob and walked into a beautiful apartment suite. Although she knew about the corner suites and could even quote the monthly fee of $8399, she had never seen the inside of one or visited with any of the more affluent residents.

A mahogany bookcase stood in the entry way, filled with classic volumes bound in gold and silver lettering. She whispered their titles, "Moby Dick," "To Kill a Mockingbird," "The Holy Bible." Shiny cream-colored flooring reflected the light that streamed in from a beveled glass transom window in the corner. Abigail gasped as she saw the black grand piano that took up most of the space in the living area. Two forest green wing chairs touched arms while a marble coffee table held a cloisonné vase filled with more yellow roses.

"Please come in, my dear. Sweet Melissa called to let me know you would be coming, and I'm steeping some tea for us. I so love having visitors. Won't you join me here in the dinette?"

Abigail's attention turned toward the sing-song voice. A woman in a peacock blue caftan turned from the stove and gracefully moved forward with her hand outstretched. A matching turban framed her face and for a moment, Abigail wondered if the woman was a cancer patient. But sprigs of white hair escaped from under the turban while one long white tendril teased the woman's shoulder. In comparison with this bright, beautiful creature, she felt like a drab winter landscape.

"Please. Won't you have a seat?" The woman motioned toward satin tapestry chairs in a warmer and richer green than the wing chairs. "My name is Ruth."

"I'm Abigail." Then she added, "My name means source of joy." For some reason, that piece of information slipped out.

Ruth pulled out her chair and seated herself with confident poise. "My dear Abigail, source of joy, what brings you to our Villa on this fine day?" Only a few crow's feet mapped the corners of Ruth's eyes, while the rest of her skin seemed translucent.

"I'm here on a mission, because I love to bake. I wanted to share these with you." She reached inside her bag and retrieved the napkin with the brownies inside.

Ruth clapped and exclaimed, "A party! How lovely! We must celebrate with music." She rose from her chair and moved toward the piano where she played a lovely arpeggio of various chords. Then she segued into a lively piece that set Abigail's feet in motion.

"What is that?"

"Mozart's Sonata in C. It keeps my fingers limber and makes me happy."

"You play beautifully."

"But it is I who must thank you for giving me the opportunity. Now, let's have our tea, shall we?"

Abigail felt as if she had stepped into another time zone as the gracious Ruth poured the tea. A cinnamon aroma filled the space. She placed a brownie on each of their tea saucers. With one bite, Ruth closed her eyes and seemed transported into that delicious place between taste and smell.

"Heavenly," she said. "I no longer bake, but my late husband would have absolutely loved these. Perhaps I should order some for my great-grandson. He loves any type of dessert, especially anything with such a rich chocolate flavor. My dear, you have a gift."

"Oh, I never take orders for my brownies or sell them. My mother and I used to make them together so it's a type of love fest whenever I bake a new batch." She wanted to tell Ruth everything about Mama, about the times they made brownies together, about her sadness whenever she thought of how Mama died. Maybe another day. "You mentioned a great-grandson. How many children do you have?"

"Ah, Obed. My sweet son, my only child was cut down during that horrid Vietnam War. He received a posthumous purple heart which was presented to his beautiful wife and their son, my grandson Jesse. It was a most bittersweet occasion, the pride I felt for my son yet the tragedy of losing him. I was fortunate he and his wife presented me with a grandson who has now greatly multiplied our family. I have eight great grandchildren and a multitude of great greats." Ruth sipped from her teacup and her pale blue eyes twinkled. "And now…you are trying to guess my age. Yes?"

Abigail's face flushed. "If you want to tell me," she said as she swallowed the last bite of her brownie, trying to hide her embarrassment.

"I am ninety-five, my dear, and you have only to study my hands to see the consequences of age. The hands, you know, always tell the truth."

Ruth once again lifted her teacup to her lips. Abigail did notice the pale thinness of Ruth's skin and the dark blue veins underneath. Brown age spots traveled up Ruth's forearm, hidden in part by the length of her caftan sleeves.

No Visible Scars

"Ninety-five? That's amazing. I would never have guessed it. How do you keep your skin so beautiful?" She felt a bit shy asking such personal questions, but Ruth did, after all, bring up the subject of aging.

"Ah, my dear, perhaps genetics. I will say, my most important beauty secret is peace."

"Peace?"

"But of course. When we are anxious, we tend to frown which causes those pesky lines in our foreheads. But when we stay in peace, the fears and anxieties have no place to land so they fly away. We are left with only a calm which soothes our souls and keeps us looking young. And of course, I spend every day with my beloved. That helps more than anything."

"Your beloved? I thought you mentioned your husband had passed."

"My beloved is my God, the divine one who resides in my soul. Since God is timeless, the closer I stay to him and the more time I spend with him, the less aged I feel. I read his book every day, the Bible, and when I play my piano, I play for him. He and I have the most lovely conversations. So I suppose he is the one who keeps me looking young." Ruth leaned closer across the table. "But of course, a little coconut oil never hurts."

Abigail giggled as Ruth laughed out loud.

"My dear, would you entertain an old woman by allowing me to show you pictures of my family?"

"Oh, yes. I'd love to see them."

Ruth pointed toward the bookcase. "Over there, if you would be so kind. The family album is a bit too heavy for me to carry these days. Third shelf, toward the middle. A gold covering. Do you see it?"

Abigail quickly spotted the album and lifted it from its place. She carefully carried it to the table and set it before Ruth, then moved her chair around the table so they could look at the album together.

Ruth caressed the cover, then opened to the first page which showed a young and breath-takingly beautiful Ruth in her wedding gown. Long black hair hung over one shoulder while a lacy veil graced her head. Next to her stood the groom, his eyes on his bride. Even in the somewhat yellowed photograph, Abigail saw the love that beamed on his face. Nate had never looked at her with such devotion.

"My wonderful Beau," Ruth said. "He was actually my second husband as my first love died a tragic and sudden death from a strange virus. His brother also succumbed to the same virus as well as their father. It was a cruel and terrible time. But my dear, let's not focus on the sadness.

"Beau and I were incredibly happy for many years." She turned the page. "And here we have our brave and gallant son, Obadiah. We called him Obed because he had such difficulty learning to pronounce his name. My goodness, he gave us so much joy. His grandmother doted on him, and he never wanted for attention."

Through the years of family photos they traveled, through birthday parties, Christmas celebrations, Easter egg hunts and graduations. Ruth described each picture, often pausing to touch a cheek or stroke a forehead, seeming to live within the past as she explained it in the present.

"And here is my beloved grandson, Jesse. Obed and his wife, Amanda, had only the one son before that dreaded war took away my boy. But now...look at this...." Ruth turned another page and showed off a photo of a large group with children like stair steps and another one asleep in a cradle.

"Jesse and his wife decided to bless me with an entire tribe of children, seven boys and two girls. Just look at these precious little ones. How I love each of them! We have celebrated a lifetime of birthday parties and graduations, baptisms and weddings. And my gracious, the laughter I bundle in my heart and carry with me all my days.

"But this one," Ruth pointed to the cradle. "This little boy, the youngest man child of the group, he grew up to own my heart. He is the one who inherited my love for music, and he writes the most beautiful poetry. Then he composes songs and places his poems within the notes. Why, my dear, you cannot even imagine how beautiful his songs are."

As Ruth continued to turn the pages, Abigail began to see the great grandchildren grow up, marry and have those great-greats Ruth talked about. But the child in the cradle, the special great grandson seemed to tug at her heart. Strange that she felt she almost knew him as he stood before her in his Cub Scout uniform, jumped off a diving board into the family pool, then stared at the camera with a mouth full of metal braces.

The years of Ruth's album continued as she flipped through the pages, pointing out each family event as if it had happened the day before. Abigail marveled at Ruth's memory, but she was talking about the people she loved most. Whenever she pointed out the special great grandson, her voice softened.

"Do you know that even now, as busy as he is, this sweet boy comes to visit me every other day. He always brings me a bouquet of yellow roses, because he knows they are my favorite. He tells me all about his business and often, he shares with me his latest poem. Sometimes he brings his guitar and we play music together. He is the treasure of my heart," Ruth stated as she turned another page.

Then suddenly Abigail understood why she felt a kinship to the childish pictures of this boy. Standing outside his first car, obviously proud and excited, stood the high school version of David. She decided not to mention that she worked with him. Better to feign ignorance and continue to page through the album.

But it was Ruth who interrupted their time together. "Oh, my dear, I suddenly find myself in need of a nap. Do you mind terribly if I retire to my bedroom? And will you promise to come visit me again?"

"Of course. Thank you so much for sharing your family pictures with me and the lovely cup of tea. It's been an honor to meet you."

"Do come again. Soon." Ruth stood and Abigail noticed the slight stoop of the shoulders, the careful placement of the hands on the back of the chair as if to steady herself.

"May I help you to your bedroom?"

"Oh, no, my dear. While I am able, I must continue to make do for myself. Please see yourself out. Good day."

She tiptoed to the entrance of Ruth's apartment and carefully shut the door behind her. Except for Jubilee, she had never met a more intriguing woman. How did women such as Jubilee and Ruth somehow manage to live such authentic and significant lives? Their marriages did not define them. Although a widow, Ruth seemed peaceful and content.

It seemed Ruth's Beau wasn't anything like Abigail's Nate. Then again, the fault wasn't entirely with the man in a woman's life. Surely she could not assign all the blame on Nate for her unhappiness. Somehow she would learn to be true to herself and content like Ruth, with or without Nate's approval.

Perhaps Jubilee would provide some answers at the next Life Limits class. Or maybe developing a relationship with Ruth would help her find her true identity. She rubbed her chest, suddenly missing Mama. Maybe a friendship with Ruth would help fill the loneliness.

As Abigail pulled out of the Villa's parking lot, she recognized the Jeep Wrangler parked two places away from the handicapped sign. She watched David get out of the driver's side. He carried a large vase of yellow roses.

She smiled. Ruth would be delighted.

No Visible Scars

CHAPTER FOURTEEN

As Nate's flight prepared for takeoff from Denver International, he loaded his bag into the luggage compartment. He knew Sam was pleased with his work and all the extra energy he invested in the sites outside the KC Metro. Their bottom line looked better since he started visiting the various locations, meeting with staff and helping them fill empty apartments.

Bring in the money. Move out the dead residents and replace them with those whose families paid plenty. Of course, he never spoke those words out loud. To live in the best place, residents and their families had to be willing to pay for it.

The motto of the company was embroidered in gold on Nate's leather briefcase. He ran his thumb over the lettering, a confident smile as he felt its nubby texture, proud of his fine work: "Villas de Comfort—The Best Place for Senior Living."

He was pleased with the new Denver site. He had produced his best pitch to potential residents and encouraged the staff. "Stay on top of your game every day," he told them. "Keep the residents happy and safe."

He settled into his seat in First Class and buckled his seat belt. Snickered as he thought about the family he had just registered for the Denver location. He had delivered one of his best spiels to the worried son. "Your father will be pleased to know he will soon be living in this beautiful setting, with the best care for senior citizens in this area. And the cuisine is excellent. We hire the best chefs, some of them trained in New York or Paris."

He could smell how close they were to inking a decision, so he used his final and most effective tool—guilt.

"It's a shame, of course, that you can't keep your father in your home. But the days of multiple families living together are long gone. At the Villas de Comfort, we understand family members have to work and can't care for their aging loved ones. Then if Alzheimer's or dementia occurs, your father will be cared for by our professional staff."

The son of the soon-to-be-resident sniffled. Nate knew he had made the sale. He waited until the man grabbed a tissue and blew his nose. He pointed to the bronze trash can in the corner of the room, and the man tossed the tissue toward it.

Missed. What a wimp! Housecleaning would take care of it.

"My father gave me everything," the man said. "I just want the best for him now."

"Of course. That's what we offer at the Villas, the very best for your dear father." He watched the new client sign the forms, shook the man's hand, then walked him to the entrance of the Villa. Another sale. Sam would be pleased.

The plane rumbled as it taxied toward the runway. Nate hoped to take a power nap. But the phrase "Dear father" plagued him. Lucky bastard to have been raised by a father who obviously cared for his kid.

He settled back as memories wandered to a little league baseball game. He had just celebrated his tenth birthday and was so proud to be standing on second base, the sand-filled bag under his cleats. He took his stance a bit left of the bag as he waited for the next batter. Then watched his father stand in the bleachers and move toward the bottom of the steps.

Probably going for some nachos and a Coke. He discovered later, his father had left the park and driven away without a word. The coach drove Nate home where he found his mother crying over a note. Something about, "Need to find myself in the big bad world...tired of the bills and the daily grind...left a little something for the kid in his bedroom."

Nate ran to his room and discovered a wad of two-dollar bills. For years, he comforted himself that although his father missed the rest of his baseball games, his induction as an Eagle scout and his high school graduation, at least he left him something meaningful.

His mother folded in on herself. One day she swallowed a bunch of pills. Nate found her on the bathroom floor, called 9-1-1, watched them do CPR, then lift her limp body onto the gurney. He stuffed his tears and called his grandparents who drove all the way from their farm in New Mabry, Missouri.

Grandpa Manon and Grandma Rita arranged everything for the funeral. They contacted Nate's father, but he never showed up. Something hard settled in Nate's chest as his mother's coffin lowered into the ground. It hardened a bit more as his grandparents cleaned out the house, packed up Nate's life in boxes and drove him to their farm.

He learned about hard work while helping Grandpa, and his grandparents helped him grow up right. They took him to the Southern Believers of the Redeemed Church where he learned to fit in with a bunch of dumb kids and follow the rules. It was easy to memorize all the Bible verses, agree to get dunked in the lake so he could take communion and be right with God. He studied hard at the New Mabry High School where twelve kids graduated in his class. The yearbook proclaimed Nathan Calebian as "Most likely to succeed."

But every night he massaged that hard knot inside and vowed, "As soon as possible, I'll leave this hick town. I'll make my first million before I'm 25 and wherever he is, my dad will be proud of me." It was dangerous to keep people close to his heart. The only thing that mattered was to own a wad of bills.

When he drove away from New Mabry and started college, he promised to never return. His grandparents sometimes visited, took him out for pizza and complained about their lumbago or too much potato salad at the last church social. As soon as they drove away, he walked to the nearest bar and downed a couple of brews. Then he found a girl and made her love him through the night.

His grandparents made their exit easy for him. They died at the same time when the old gas generator exploded and burned the farmhouse down. His entire history a pile of ashes. Nate sold all the farm equipment at an auction and made a small fortune when he persuaded a developer to buy the land.

As he deposited the money in his Capital One account, he whispered, "You'd be proud of me, Dad. I've grown that bunch of bills you gave me."

When he met Dave in Econ 101, they hit it off. During finals week their junior year, they planned how to turn their ideas into a business venture and formulated the demographics for an assisted living facility.

After they earned their MBA's, Nate used part of his inheritance from the farm sale to bankroll their first office. Dave attracted the prosperous and important people, especially the wives of wealthy investors. Nate didn't care. He already had his trophy wife in Abigail.

He knew she wanted to work with kids, but he would never allow it. Whenever she mentioned kids, a memory haunted him—a young boy standing on second base while his father drove away. That boulder inside grew larger.

The thump of the landing gear reminded him to text Abby. "Pick me up at the Delta gate. Ten minutes."

He didn't like this new version of Abby. Every Wednesday night, a crafts class. "Some secret project, especially for him," she said. It was a stupid idea. He hated when she came home all happy and smug. Sometimes Abby

No Visible Scars

and Cass stayed in the car and gabbed for an hour after she was supposed to be in the house. What were they talking about anyway?

Abby's purpose was to find her significance in being his spouse, to meet his needs and submit to his commands. He learned that in New Mabry. Whenever Grandpa Manon wanted something, he yelled at Grandma Rita, "Woman, submit." She bowed her head and did what he commanded her to do.

He would accept no less.

"Thank you for flying with us," the flight attendant said.

Nate stood to retrieve his bag. He hurried through the passageway and toward the exit doors. Where was his woman? She was supposed to be waiting for him. He watched as other passengers met their families. Hugs. Kisses. He massaged his chest.

The Acura swung next to the curb. The trunk swung open, and he loaded his bag. He slammed the trunk shut and hurried to the driver's side.

"Get out," he said through the half-opened window. "I'll drive."

Abby frowned, but opened the door and slid out of her seat. He grabbed her arm, pulled her to him and planted a hard kiss on her mouth. To remind her he was in control and what he expected as soon as they got home.

She didn't kiss him back, but quickly moved behind the car and into the passenger seat. He blasted the horn at the slow-moving cab in front of him, then swerved to the left and toward the airport exit.

"Did you have a nice flight?" Abby asked.

"Yeah. No problems. The new site in Colorado is on target for a successful launch. We're full up already with a waiting list."

"That's wonderful," she said. But her voice sounded kind of flat.

"I'm hungry for a sandwich. Let's go to Quizno's."

"All right. I could use a salad."

She said nothing more, but Nate glanced at her every time they stopped at a red light. She seemed a little more upright, as if she was working on her posture. It suited her, although he wondered what she'd been doing all weekend. "You and Cass been doing more of those craft things?"

"Only on Wednesday nights. Actually, I've met the most amazing woman at the Villa in Overland Park."

"Yeah? So what?"

"You told me to take my brownies over there, so I did. The director told me about the woman in the corner suite. Her name is Ruth."

"Dave's great grandmother."

"You've met her?"

"No, but I know everything about the Villas. Dave visits her, and she lives in the most expensive suite we own. She's got loads of money. He's got a big family. They do stuff together all the time." With his right fist, he massaged that suffocating rock in his chest. "What's so great about Ruth?"

"She's just so real. So authentic. She appreciates everyone she meets, including me."

"Authentic?" He groaned. "That sounds like some mumbo jumbo feminist stuff. Don't start getting any weird ideas."

She looked out the window, away from his statement. He steered into Quizno's parking lot, then shut off the motor and got out of the car. She seemed to take her sweet time joining him at the door.

"Hurry up. I've got some things to do tonight before I hit the sheets. We've got a meeting in the morning with Sam."

Neither of them spoke during the meal. When they finished, Abby picked up all their trash and deposited it in the bins while Nate refilled his Coke. In the car, he belched loudly then said, "I've decided you don't need to make me any dumb craft thing. I want you to stop going to that class on Wednesday nights."

"Stop going? Nate, please, no. I can't. I really enjoy it, and...well, I'm doing it for you." She stroked his arm.

He shrugged away. "Forget it. Like I said, I don't need any stupid old craft and you can do more things at home."

"Like what? We have a maid and I always finish my work at the office. Besides, Cassie and I really enjoy going to...crafts class. Cassie's husband lets her go."

"I don't care what that dimwit does with his wife. You're my woman, and I say you're done. No more Wednesday nights out." He scowled. "You need to be home with me, every night."

"But Nate...."

"I said, you're done. No more. That's it." He slapped the steering wheel.

As he swung onto the ramp toward I-35 south, he heard her sniffle. He didn't care. Let her cry about it. The typical woman thing to do.

A whimper. Then she said, "Can't I finish this one project? Please, Nate. It's only a couple more weeks. Then I'll be done. You're the one who always says we should finish with excellence."

"This isn't the same as finishing at work. This is just a bunch of women doing stuff that doesn't mean anything."

"But it isn't just a bunch of women. These are my friends and some of them you know. Cassie and…uh…Samuel's wife…Roberta."

"Sam's wife is in this group?"

"Well…yes. Didn't I mention that before?"

"No, you did not." He needed to think about this for a minute. If Sam's wife was part of the group, then it would look bad if Abby dropped out. He didn't want Sam getting wind of it and thinking he didn't support his wife. Sam was always talking about the importance of family relationships. Plus, the board was still talking about who would take Saul's place as CEO. He was the number one choice, and he didn't want to screw that up. Maybe Abby could help him get in good with Roberta who would tell Sam and then his promotion would be secure.

He punched the garage door opener and parked the Acura next to his Lexus. Popped the trunk and lifted out his bag, then followed Abby into the house.

"Okay," he said. "You can keep going to this craft class. While you're there, try to pal up with Roberta. Make sure she knows I'm letting you attend and tell her good stuff about me."

"Of course, Nate. I would never imply anything but good about you." She turned toward him, her smile sweet and her eyes still misty from the tears. She really was a good-looking piece of meat. She would never dare abandon him or do anything against his wishes. He had spent the last nine years of his life training her.

He grabbed her around the waist and held her close, then bit her ear lobe. She shivered, and he knew she wanted him. Why wait until bedtime? He lifted her over his shoulder like a sack of potatoes and trudged up the stairs. She would show her gratitude for his generous decision to let her stay in the class, and he would win all the way around. She would satisfy his needs and pave the way for his next move up the corporate ladder.

CHAPTER FIFTEEN

"You said what? You told him Roberta is in our class?" Cassie's eyes widened as she sipped her seltzer water at the Happy Grounds Cafe.

"I know. It was a stretch, but I had to do something. He wasn't going to let me go to class anymore. I can't stop now, not when I'm learning so much." Abigail bit into a blueberry scone and licked her lips. Turbinado sugar on top, a nice crunch of extra flavor.

"And you never thought about telling Nate what you're really doing and that he can't stop you...period?"

"Are you kidding? Do you know what he would do to me if I demanded something like that?"

The spew of the espresso machine at the bar drowned out Cassie's response. Abigail leaned forward. "What?"

"Aren't we learning about this in class? That we have the freedom to say what we feel, to do what protects our own hearts. Isn't that what Jubilee would say?"

Abigail sighed. "Probably. Hey, I didn't say I was perfect, and I *am* still learning all this stuff. It's just that...well...Nate is so difficult and...sometimes I don't know what to do."

Cassie frowned. "Are you sure this isn't an abusive situation? I mean, really...the way he treats you. Why do you put up with it?"

"Because I have no choice, and abuse is such a strong word. I hate to call it that. He's my husband and he's my financial security, and well...I guess I deserve it sometimes."

"Deserve it? That's not true." Cassie put her hand over Abigail's. "Wasn't it last week when Jubilee shared that list of abusive traits? Wait! I think I still have it in my bag." She rummaged through her collection of swirly Post-it notes and a couple of lipstick containers. "Yep. Here it is. Listen to this and see if any of these describe your dear husband." Cassie unfolded the paper and read, "'Uses intimidation to make her afraid.'"

"Check."

"'Puts her down or mocks her opinions.'"

"Check again." She massaged her neck, tried to work out the tension.

"'Makes her feel guilty.' Hmm, you did just said you deserved it. And here's a big one, 'He controls what she does.'" Cassie rolled her eyes. "Control. Like saying you can't go to class."

"Well, to be fair, Nate doesn't *know* it's a Life Limits class. He'd really blow a gasket if he knew the truth."

"My point exactly." Cassie read on, "'Makes all the decisions, treats her like a servant,' and then of course the obvious, 'punching, hitting, raping, hair pulling, et cetera.'"

Abigail touched the spot on her head where Nate had yanked her hair. He hadn't pulled her hair since. Maybe he didn't really mean to.

Cassie folded up the paper. "So...don't one or more of these describe Nate? Should you set a difficult boundary? Get away for a while?"

"I'd love to, but Nate would never allow a separation. Any type of scandal might affect the company. Samuel and the board of directors are big on family and on keeping marriages together and well...that would destroy everything. Besides, where would I go? I don't have any friends except you. If I hid out with you and Rick, Nate would figure it out right away. I really don't have any legal reason. I mean...he doesn't hit me. And the church? What would the church people say? Everyone would blame me, because Nate's such a model citizen. What would I do? Where would I work? How would I get the money? Everything I have and everything I am is connected with Nate."

Cassie sipped her water while a frown formed on her forehead. "Yeah, I get what you're saying. But aren't these a bunch of excuses to protect this man? What about protecting yourself and your dreams? Don't you count for more than what Nate allows you to be?"

Abigail felt her heart thump. "You really think I should leave him?"

"I'm saying do something to protect yourself." She touched Abigail's hand. "I know that sounds harsh, but what good are friends if they don't tell you the truth? Listen. I just want you to be safe. Surely you know that."

Abigail's stomach roiled. "I have to go to the restroom. I think I'm going to throw up."

Her heart pounded, and her neck muscles felt as if they might explode. She ran to the ladies room. Both stalls were busy. She leaned over the sink and lost her lunch. She turned on the water faucet and watched the debris slowly swirl around and down the drain.

A woman came out of the nearest stall. "Everything all right, honey? Do you need some help?"

Abigail shook her head. "I'm fine now. Thanks." She hurried into the emptied stall and locked the door, then pulled down her pants and sat on the toilet. Held her head in her hands.

Cassie was her best friend. She needed Cassie as the one person with whom she could vent and have fun shopping. But now Cassie seemed disappointed in how she was handling life with Nate. On top of everything else, she couldn't lose her only friend.

With the baby coming, Cassie also needed her. Abigail wanted to squirt little blue or pink frosting booties on cupcakes and invite lots of women to a baby shower, maybe even the women from class.

Maybe it *was* time to leave Nate or at least threaten to leave him. Other women did it. They escaped from abusive situations and found places of refuge. She had seen a number for such a place on the pamphlets Jubilee had given her. The pamphlets she trashed at Sonic. She slapped the toilet paper roll, disgusted with herself.

But Nate wasn't mean all the time. He hadn't done all those things Cassie had read. Sometimes he held her hand when they watched a movie together. That made her feel loved and safe. Maybe the pressure at the office caused him to yell at her and call her names.

What was it Jubilee said one night? Women fall into the cycle of abuse and feel powerless to stop it. Women live in denial, afraid to face the truth. Something like that.

Did she just throw up a bunch of denial in the bathroom sink? She pulled some toilet paper and wiped her face, then blew her nose.

A slight rap on the stall door and Cassie's voice, "You okay, girlfriend?"

"Yeah, sure. Just finishing up. I'll be out in a minute."

Cassie rapped on the door again. "Hurry up, because I'm really craving a hot fudge sundae, and I heard about this new place that has all natural ingredients. I figure we can buy a large sundae and split it."

Abigail stood up and flushed the stool. "Sure. Great idea."

On the way out to her car, Cassie squeezed Abigail around the waist. "So you'll think about what I said, right? Set some boundaries with Nate?"

Abigail nodded. "Yes. I'm going to figure this out. I have to somehow save my life without sabotaging my soul."

Cassie giggled. "You know who you sound like?"

They looked at each other and both said, "Jubilee."

༄༄༄

After Nate fell asleep, she padded downstairs for a peach mango yogurt. Swirled it around, then spooned a big dollop into her mouth. The citrusy smell brought a smile. She bit into a mango and power-fisted the ceiling. Time for some investigative work.

No Visible Scars

She powered up the computer and typed in the password: NaibelaC32. Their last name in reverse, Nate's initial and his age. His secure code to prevent hackers. Every year on his birthday, he changed the last number to match his age. He always used his own identity. It was always about Nate.

She researched local colleges and the costs of tuition. Imagined herself walking from class to class, eventually marching proudly across the stage to accept her teaching degree. The first day in her own classroom, pixie faces upturned as she sounded out the alphabet. A wonderful dream.

She crept to the bottom of the steps and listened for any sounds from upstairs. Nothing. Then she Googled places for women to stay when they were in danger. A few locations popped up, always without an address. "Of course," she whispered. "Extra security." Every organization required a police escort, a call to 9-1-1. She had already tried that route with Officer Tamara. Any faith-based locations? Churches that might help? None.

She shut down the computer and sat for a while, staring at the black screen. At least she could tell Cassie she had tried. Maybe trying another boundary would make it clear to Nate. She would have to think about her next step. Something had to change.

CHAPTER SIXTEEN

On Monday, Samuel called the office. Abigail answered and started to switch the call to Nate's phone, but Samuel said, "No. Just tell Nathan and David that the board members and I will be in the office at two o'clock today. Sorry for the short notice, but I've just met with Saul and confirmed we're moving forward with another leader."

"Yes, sir," Abigail said. This was it—the moment Nate had waited for. Soon, her husband would become the next CEO of the Villas de Comfort. Her stomach fluttered with a mass of nervous hope. What would this promotion mean for her? Maybe Nate would hire a second assistant. Then she would have the freedom to take a few classes toward her degree.

"And Abigail," Samuel continued, "as we're making some changes, I want you to know how much we appreciate your fine work at the front desk. Everyone is impressed with how you conduct yourself. We'll see you this afternoon."

"Thank you, sir." Yes, she was the perfect executive assistant and performed her job well. But Samuel might think differently if she blew the whole "family-friendly" ideal of the Villas and set difficult boundaries with Nate.

But this was no time for distractions. Nate and David needed to be told about the meeting so they could prepare information, spreadsheets and anything else the board might want to review.

She hurried toward Nate's corner office and rapped on the door.

"Yeah?"

She entered quietly. Nate hated to be disturbed if he was in the middle of something. He sat in the leather chair, a pile of papers in his hand and a frown on his face. Two twenty-four inch computer monitors flanked his glass-topped desk.

He glanced up. "What do you want? I'm busy."

"Samuel just called. He and the board members will be here this afternoon at two o'clock. He indicated they had made a decision about Saul."

He jumped from his chair as his frown turned to a grin. "It's finally going to happen. I'm going to be the next CEO. I can feel it in my bones. Quick! We've got to get the last annual report ready. Print off copies for everyone. Make sure we have enough of everything in the conference room. Do you have some brownies?"

"No. I don't have time to bake them, and I don't have all the ingredients anyway."

"Next time, be more prepared. This is what we pay you for, to be ready for anything. Never mind. Go over to that deli down the street and buy some pastries, something Sam might like. Use petty cash. Have you told David yet?"

"No. I thought you would want to know first."

"Good. Go tell him and then get the pastries. Then hurry back and get busy on that report. Forget about taking lunch today."

She turned to leave, but Nate hurried around his desk and grabbed her elbow. His fingernails bit into her flesh. "Don't tell Dave or Sam that I'm expecting this promotion. Sam's big on humility. He wouldn't want me thinking I'm the right man for the job even though we both know I am. Got it?"

"Of course." She rubbed her elbow as she hurried out of Nate's office. No time now to set a boundary such as, "Don't ever grab my arm like that again."

As she hurried toward David's office, she heard the strum of his guitar. For a moment, she wanted to stand outside the door and listen to the soft melody. David was humming. She hated to interrupt, but she knew Nate wanted her to hurry and get everything prepared.

She knocked softly.

"Come in." David stood in the corner of his office, flanked by a ficus tree and a bongo drum. He strummed his guitar softly, moving from one chord to the other. When he looked up, he smiled. "Hey there. You want to hear my latest tune? I'm trying to decide how to fit one of my poems into this progression." He fingered through a few measures. "No, that doesn't sound right."

She sighed. "It sounds wonderful to me." She felt the stress of the day fade. So different from being with Nate in his office.

On a corner table, photos of his large family reflected light. Tiny frames with little children in funny poses. If she took the time to look, one of the photos might include Ruth's lovely face staring back at her.

David seemed to read her mind. "I wanted to thank you for visiting my great grandmother. She told me about this lovely woman who came for tea and gave her the best brownies she had ever eaten. I figured it must be you."

"It was entirely my pleasure. Ruth is such a delightful person. It was an honor to meet her." She smiled at the thought of her new friend. "I hate to interrupt your music, but you have a meeting with Samuel and the board members this afternoon at two o'clock. Nate wants all the information on the last annual report and anything else you think needs to be added."

"Oh, sure," he said. "I'll email you all the info." He laid his guitar on the leather love seat. "I suppose Samuel's going to announce Nate's promotion. That's good. The Villas really need to move forward and stop waiting for Saul to get with the program."

"You know about the promotion?"

"Yeah. It's been coming for a while, and I'm glad for Nate. He deserves it. He's worked hard, and so have you. We appreciate your work. I'm sorry if we don't tell you that often enough."

She felt a warm blush. "Thank you. I need to buy some pastries for the meeting, then I'll get right to that paperwork."

"I'm sure everything will be fine. Will we have some of your brownies?"

"Not enough time to make them."

She hurried out of David's office, wishing she could sit a while and listen to his music. As she rounded the corner hallway, she almost collided with Nate. His coffee cup sloshed on her black blazer.

"Ouch!"

"Look what you've done," he said. "If that coffee had spilled on my shirt, I'd have to change before the meeting. Did you tell Dave about this afternoon?"

"Yes." As she swiped her wet blazer, she hoped for an apology but knew it wouldn't come. "I'm on my way to order the pastries. I'll be back soon."

"Hurry up. Everything has to be just right and in place when they get here. I've got to talk to Dave a minute." He hurried past her and toward the sound of a strumming guitar. "I wish he'd stop playing that infernal music in the office."

As she stepped into the deli, her stomach growled. If only she had enough time to sit outside under one of the umbrellas, sip a mocha or bite into some fresh pumpernickel bread. But she knew Nate wanted her back at the office.

She settled on five of the biscotti, two bear claws and a handful of poppy seed mini-muffins. Then three macaroons, a plate full of petit fours with tiny green leaves on the frosting and a couple of Napoleons. Maybe some of the deli's brownies. No. Samuel preferred hers. At the last minute, she grabbed a container of peach yogurt then stuck a tube of string cheese in the basket for lunch at her desk. No matter what Nate said, she needed some protein to make it through the afternoon.

Back at the office, she unloaded the goodies on the conference room table. Fortunately, the corporation always kept beautiful linens in the mahogany hutch that filled the south end of the conference room. She pulled out a periwinkle blue satin cloth and immediately thought of Ruth. She would look stunning in that fabric. Abigail wondered how that color would look next to her own skin and for a moment, she played with the silky softness, running it over her arms.

With the pastries arranged artfully on crystal plates, the coffee cups laid out and the Keurig filled, she hurried back to her desk to finish printing out the reports. By the time she checked for errors, punched holes in all the pages and laid them inside the gold binders, it was almost 1:45. She quickly tore into the tube of string cheese, bit off a couple of bites, then spooned into the yogurt.

After her quickie lunch, she checked her lip gloss. As she placed her compact back in her purse, she heard the ding of the elevator. Samuel and Larry Cox, the VP of the board, entered the front office together. Already in deep conversation, they barely acknowledged her although Samuel smiled briefly in her direction.

Nate came out of his office, his suit coat buttoned and his silk red power tie in a perfect Windsor knot. David also joined the group, looking more casual with his blue polo shirt and khakis. Soon the other board members arrived: Sylvia Anderson, owner of a chain of boutiques in the Kansas City Metro, Cole Stanton, one of the assistant coaches for the Kansas City Chiefs, looking oddly out of place in a power suit, Drew Comcast, a top-selling realtor who specialized in corporate realty and sometimes advertised on Fox 4 News, Linda Patterson, the director of the Villas de Comfort in Prairie Village and Cao and Si Chin who hoped to open a franchise of the Villas in Beijing.

Abigail brewed coffee and poured water. She made sure everyone's needs were met before she closed the conference room door and headed back to her desk. She rolled her neck, trying to ease the tension and hoped for his sake and also for hers, everything would go smoothly for Nate. She worked on some of the monthly charts. Point and click. Point and click.

Barely thirty minutes later, the conference door opened and the board members filed out. They wished her a good day, all of them smiling, obviously happy with the results of the meeting.

She heard Samuel say, "You'll do fine, son. We have all the confidence in the world you're going to help this company move forward. Let me know if you have any questions. Let's have a celebration here at HQ in a week or so, to announce your promotion."

Samuel, David and Nate rounded the corner. As Samuel shook hands all around, Nate looked pale. His mouth was set in one of those straight lines that meant he was trying to impress someone but his heart wasn't in it. David looked a bit shocked, his face almost as red as Nate's tie.

Samuel approached her desk. "Well, my dear, meet the new CEO of the Villas de Comfort. David has been chosen to succeed Saul, and we know he'll do a masterful job. He's such a great communicator and seems to find the common bond between staff, board members and residents.

"Your husband, of course, will receive a bonus with some additional duties as the Development Officer and COO. And you as well, my dear. We did not forget you. You'll receive a nice bonus and an increase in your annual wage."

"Thank you. I appreciate your encouragement."

Again Samuel shook hands with David and Nate, then saluted Abigail on his way out of the office. To his credit, Nate tried to act like the better man. He slapped David on the shoulder and said, "Way to go, buddy. You did it."

David shook his head. "I didn't see this coming, Nate. I never expected this. It should have been you."

"Well, it isn't me. So buck up and do your best for the company. I'll help you however I can."

David shook his head again and wandered back down the hallway to his office. The muscles worked in Nate's jaw.

"I don't want to be disturbed," he said. "Got it? No calls. No interruptions. We'll talk tonight."

She nodded. "I'm so sorry, Nate. You must be...."

"Shut up. I don't want to hear it." He stormed away and slammed his door.

She walked into the conference room and surveyed the unopened binders, the pastries mostly untouched. A few cupcake papers from the mini-muffins lay on the blue satin tablecloth and only two coffee mugs had been used. She quickly washed them, gathered up the rest of the pastries and put them in the fridge. Then she wrapped up one of the Napoleons to take home for Nate. Maybe that would help him feel better.

She could only imagine how he would deal with his anger. Now was not the time to set a boundary of any kind. Now was the time to merely survive.

No Visible Scars

CHAPTER SEVENTEEN

David planned to stay at the office until midnight. How in the world had this crazy thing happened? When Samuel had announced his name as the new CEO, David looked quickly at Nate. His buddy looked like he was about to stroke out, and his pointer finger tapped the table.

"Oh, God, I don't want to be the Chief Executive Officer of the Villas. All I want is to play my music, write poetry and get to know Michele a little better. This doesn't make sense."

Of course, he wanted to continue to work at the Villas, but only in a supportive role with Nate, not as the head guy of a huge corporation. He had already planned his next trip to Africa in a couple of months to help drill water wells for his personal mission. And he worried about Granny Ruth and her health. Now he had to take on this massive job and keep the business going in the right direction, maybe internationally.

He shook his head, then sang through the chorus of his latest composition. "You are my refuge and my strength. I cling to you, held by your powerful right hand."

He was going to need all of God's strength and then some in the weeks ahead. As he heard Nate's office door slam, he could imagine what Nate was thinking. He knew his college buddy's eagerness for the top job and his plans to turn the Villas into a successful Fortune 500 company, much bigger than the Midwest area they now occupied. Nate had probably sketched out his goals for the next year, along with charts on how to execute those goals and measure the success in monthly increments. He would have been a better fit for CEO. But Samuel and the board had not chosen Nate.

David pulled out a binder from his file cabinet. He flipped through it and marveled at the pictures of all the Villas. Hundreds of seniors living in safety and beauty. Maybe pushing a thousand. He would need to check on all the staff members, make sure all the residents felt comfortable, encourage their families. So much to do. His head spun with all the tasks he needed to accomplish.

He picked up a family picture and talked to the image of Granny Ruth. "But I'll still find time to visit you."

His cell phone played a chorus of "Amazing Grace," and he glanced at the caller ID. Michele. "Hey there, darlin'. Where do you want to go tonight?"

"David...I've just had a conversation with Daddy. I understand Samuel replaced him. Fired him actually." He knew that tone of voice, like fingernails on a chalkboard.

"Well, that's true, honey, but I had nothing to do with that. In fact, it was a complete surprise to me." Okay, that wasn't entirely true. He suspected Saul wasn't doing his job, but he definitely didn't expect to become the next CEO.

"In light of that decision, you'll understand I don't want to have anything to do with the Villas de Comfort. And that includes a relationship with you."

"But Michele...."

"Goodbye, David."

Terrific! Another relationship shriveled up like the rivers of Kenya. One of the side effects of occupying the corner office. He picked up a paper clip and straightened it, then crunched it into a useless mess and tossed it in the trash. He would have to go it alone for a while. Some other girl would come along. Still, he thought Michelle might be the one. He had been thinking about settling down, maybe starting a family.

Nate sure hit a home run when he found Abigail. He probably didn't know how lucky he was to have a wife who supported him and represented the company so well, sat at that front desk every day and worked so efficiently.

Lately, though, he had noticed a tired look in Abigail's eyes. Maybe she needed a vacation from the front desk or maybe they were asking her to do too much. He picked up his cell phone. Note to Abigail: ask about her job and how to make it better.

He picked up his guitar and strummed a few chords. He tried again to locate the exact tune for his latest poem, "Like the stately mountains, righteous in your might. Mercy as the heavens, faithful day and night. Clouds that billow upward...."

He heard a quiet rap on his door. Not now. Not in the middle of this phrase. He was just finding the bridge from one movement to another. Dang it! He was CEO now. Guess he had to act like it and tend to business. "Come in."

Abigail stuck her head around the door frame. "Sorry to bother you. That was a beautiful tune." She held out her steno pad. "Samuel wanted me to get the date secured for the party, to celebrate the changes happening at Corporate. What about next Saturday night at 7:30? Does that fit with your calendar?"

He picked up his phone and scrolled through it. "Yeah. That date's clear with me. Have you asked Nate?"

"No. I thought I should ask you first, now that you're the CEO."

"Abigail, this wasn't my idea. I'm sorry. The position should have gone to Nate."

She walked farther into the office, then made sure the door shut behind her. "I'm sure Nate is disappointed, but as I've thought about it…you do have a better…uhm…way with people. That's important for the CEO of an organization."

"Yeah, that's what Samuel said in the meeting. Nate has the economic smarts and knows how to make the financials work, but evidently, I'm the people person. I'm just overwhelmed with the whole idea. You'll help me, won't you? By the way, I've been wanting to ask you…do you like working here at Corporate? Anything we can do to make it easier for you?"

She hesitated, and he wondered what she was thinking behind those gorgeous amber eyes with their golden flecks. She squared back her shoulders and faced him. A tiny smile played with the dimple on her right cheek. "Since you asked, I'll tell you the truth. No. I don't like my job. It was never my dream to sit in front a computer, to point the curser and click, day after day after day."

"So what's your dream? What do you want to do?"

"Teach little children. I've always wanted to become a school teacher. That was the direction I was going before I met Nate."

"A teacher." She stood before his desk, almost humble, as if she was baring a part of her soul, some private place no one else saw. "So why don't you go back to school and finish your degree? What's keeping you from it? Surely not the finances. Nate makes enough to pay for tuition, books and anything else you'd need. Plus nowadays, you can do it all online."

She seemed to shrink a little. The dimple disappeared and a sadness darkened her eyes. "It's not the right time. Nate needs me here. Maybe someday…." She turned to leave while he fought a desire to jump around the desk and take her in his arms.

He reminded himself she was Nate's wife. "When you decide it's the right time to move toward your teaching degree, let me know. Even though you're wonderfully efficient, I'm sure we could find another executive assistant. Everyone should have a chance to pursue whatever they're created to do. Remember that, okay?"

She turned slightly and murmured, "Thanks." Then she opened the door and quickly exited.

He smiled at the thought of little kids, all huddled around Abigail, asking questions and showing her their crayon sketches. He always loved playing with his nieces and nephews.

He wanted to pick up his guitar again and find the rest of that tune he had been working on, but first—why not go visit Granny Ruth and tell her about his promotion. She would gush all over him. Then she would reassure him that he could do this great task and serve as the top guy at the Villas.

He speed-dialed a number on his phone. "Florence, this is David Judah. Do you have some yellow roses today? Great! I'll drive by in a few minutes and pick them up. Yes. Let's do a full dozen. I'm celebrating with my great grandmother."

As he grabbed his keys and started down the hallway, he heard a commotion in Nate's office. Without knocking, he opened Nate's door.

Papers and binders were strewn all over the floor. Abigail was on her knees picking them up. Nate stood over his desk, his arms supporting him and his face red.

"What's going on here?" David asked.

Nate stood upright and his hands balled into fists. "None of your business, Dave. Just because you're the CEO doesn't mean you can barge into my office."

"That may be true, but if you've got a beef, take it up with me. Not with our executive assistant." He bent down, grabbed a sheaf of papers and handed them to Abigail. She didn't even look up. He wanted to offer her a hand and help her off her knees, but she scooted away from him and kept gathering binders, papers and what David now recognized as Nate's smashed coffee cup.

"Fine," Nate said. "Let's get this out in the open and deal with it."

"In my office," said David.

Nate quickly stormed down the hallway. David followed him, tossed his keys on his desk and turned to face his friend and partner. Hopefully, he wouldn't have to settle this with his fists. Nate stood a good head above him, but David knew he was in better shape. He ran laps every day around the local school track and worked out at the company gym, one of the ways he communicated with other employees. When you sweat with people, you get to know them.

Now he watched Nate pace up and down his office, growing redder with each step.

"Take it easy, buddy," David said. "No need to have a coronary."

"It should have been mine. I've worked hard for this promotion, and you know it. I'm the one who puts together all the numbers and all the development. I'm the one who knows how to make the money work. We decided that from the beginning. This isn't fair."

"I know, but the board made this decision. We have to respect their choice and make the best of it. We can still work together as partners. I'll expect you to keep on top of the finances and move us closer to the international markets. Can't you do that, even without the title and the position you wanted?"

Nate crossed his arms. "I wanted it all, and I think I wanted it more than you. Am I right?"

David hesitated. No reason to share all his thoughts or admit he wasn't exactly thrilled with his new position. He was, after all, Nate's superior now. Some workplace boundary needed to exist between himself and his employees, even someone as close to him as Nate. "We both want what's best for the Villas and that's what counts. Isn't that so?"

"Of course. I just thought...."

"Amazing Grace" vibrated on David's phone. He checked the ID but decided not to talk to Florence right now. He quickly texted her, "Be right there."

David moved toward Nate and clapped him on the shoulder. "Listen, I've got a meeting." He checked his watch. "Why don't you and Abigail clock out early? Go home and debrief or take her out for a nice dinner, anything to get your mind off what happened. We can talk about it tomorrow. Okay?"

Nate shrugged. "Yeah. At least the Villas are still moving toward growth."

"You bet. And you're a major player, no matter what title is behind your name." He grabbed his keys and jangled them. "I'm outta' here."

On his way out of the office, David smiled at Abigail. She straightened a few papers at her desk. "Call it a day, Abigail. Go home and relax. I'll see you tomorrow. And thanks for everything."

"You're welcome," she said, but she seemed a bit preoccupied. David wondered again about the scene in Nate's office. It wasn't any of his business how a husband and wife related to each other, but he didn't want his executive assistant groveling on the floor. Everybody needed to be shown respect, to be valued for their work and dedication. That was a policy he would definitely underscore as the new CEO.

CHAPTER EIGHTEEN

As they dressed for the big celebration, Abigail hesitated inside her walk-in closet. Such a big space, filled with the clothes she hated. She wondered what Ruth's closet looked like. Probably full of colorful scarves, kaftans and the funky little shoes she always wore, some of them beaded, others with tiny ribbons sewn together. Ruth would be aghast at the boring closet that housed Abigail's clothes. Drab. Black and beige.

She grabbed the hanger for her silk black pants and scooped up the black patent heels she always wore with her "party" pants. Some party. Nate was still mad that he held the second place spot. The last two nights when he came home from work, he drank too much. Then it was an evening full of "Is this all you could think of for dinner?" and "Doesn't Sam understand everything I do for the company?" He paced through the house, banged cabinets and threw papers on the floor. "Pick those up," he demanded.

She tried to placate him. "Of course, they know all you do for the Villas. You're brilliant at your job."

"Obviously, your opinion doesn't matter."

No Visible Scars

Forget about Nate. Think about the party. Try to enjoy the evening. She reached for her black blazer and the white satiny top she knew Nate wanted her to wear. Then she remembered the sack at the back of her underwear drawer, the sack she hid after the last time she and Cassie shopped.

Cassie started to hide the sack at her house, but Abigail stopped her. "I need to take charge of my life, by setting some boundaries about what I wear. You keep my special dress and my wig, but I'm taking this first step."

"You go, girl!"

This was the time. Nate was already angry, so it couldn't get much worse. If she handled it just right, if she manipulated him instead of the other way around.... She thought for a minute. Yes, that was it. She knew what to do.

She smiled at her reflection in the mirror. She would compromise and wear the black pants and the black blazer. But underneath, something she loved.

Carefully, she pulled the peacock blue tank top out of the sack. She had fallen in love with the color as she and Cassie walked through Macy's. This beautiful piece of clothing would remind her of her friend, the brave and gracious Ruth who always shone with inner beauty. Tonight Abigail would share in that sisterhood and begin to love herself.

She wrapped her hair on top of her head and adjusted her diamond stud earrings. Nate gave her the diamonds one year at Christmas, then demanded she wear them to the annual party in their home. Tonight they reflected the color of the peacock blue. Make Nate happy by wearing the jewelry he gave her yet demand he respect her decision on the tank top. That's how business was done—through compromise. She would beat him at his own game.

As she descended the curving staircase, Nate waited at the bottom. He stared as she grew closer. A frown creased his forehead. "What are you doing in that outfit? Where did you get that thing?"

"Cassie and I found it at Macy's, on sale so it didn't cost much. I thought the color was pretty. Don't you think it's pretty, Nate?" She sidled up to him, hoping to distract him with her Elizabeth Arden cologne. "I've decided to wear this top on purpose tonight."

"I didn't give you permission to buy anything new or wear something different. We're not celebrating tonight. This is Dave's party. You don't need to look like you're enjoying it. Go take off that thing and put on something you usually wear. And hurry up."

"Exactly the point. If we look like we're celebrating with David, then we'll appear as if we're in agreement with Samuel and the board, a consensus with their decision. That will make them feel even more grateful for how you've handled things. Don't you see? We'll put one over on them because they'll never know how disappointed you were with their decision. They'll respect your humility and your leadership abilities."

Nate raised one eyebrow.

She continued to smile at him, hoping he wouldn't notice how her hands shook.

Finally, he nodded and said, "Hmm. You may have something there. Act like we're in agreement so they'll respect me even more. I like it. That's a good idea."

He pecked her on the cheek. "Maybe you're finally earning your keep." He grabbed her elbow and headed for the garage. "Come on. Let's go."

"Just a minute. I'll meet you in the car. I have to get my brownies. Samuel would have a fit if I didn't bring some." She hurried into the kitchen and reached for the crystal plate filled with her treats. The chocolate aroma engulfed her senses and her stomach growled. She remembered she hadn't eaten supper.

Glancing toward the front foyer to make sure Nate was headed toward the garage, she slipped her cell phone out of her purse and quickly took a selfie. Then she texted Cassie, "I did it!"

A reply text came back almost immediately with a big smiley face on the screen.

※※※

At the party, all the corporate employees and board directors blended into one happy group. Samuel greeted the employees and complimented them about their work.

Abigail expected David to be accompanied by Michele. But instead, Ruth appeared with him, her frail hands linked around David's forearm.

Abigail quickly moved through the crowd to greet Ruth. "It's wonderful to see you here," she said. "I'm so glad you came to celebrate with David."

"Oh, my dear, I wouldn't have missed it for the world. My great grandson the Chief Executive Officer of a corporation. The entire family is thrilled." Ruth stepped away from David and touched Abigail's arm. "And what is this? Such a beautiful top you have on tonight, my dear. Much different from what you usually wear. The color suits you."

"Thank you. I decided to be more festive tonight and wear something that made me feel...I don't know...more attractive. You've helped me realize the importance of color."

"But my dear, do you have any idea how beautiful you are? And that color just adds to your radiance. You must wear that top more often."

Abigail wished she could comply with Ruth's comment, but she knew this night was special, like Cinderella at the ball. Next week, she would return to her usual drab clothing, climb out of her pumpkin coach and work at the job she was hired to do. Point and click. Point and click.

But at least, for this night, she felt proud of herself. She had set a boundary and decided what to wear. She defied Nate's wishes, but she did it without making him mad. She stepped a bit closer to finding her true identity and being herself. Gratitude for Ruth's compliment warmed her. Jubilee would surely be proud of her.

Samuel tried to get everyone's attention, but the corporate offices were jammed with people. He motioned toward David who stuck his thumb and his forefinger in his mouth and produced a loud whistle. Everyone stopped talking and stared at Samuel who raised his glass of champagne.

"We are here tonight to celebrate another fiscal year of success, but also to announce a slight change in the corporate structure. I am proud to announce that David Judah will now act as the Chief Executive Officer of the Villas de Comfort."

Although Abigail knew the corporate grapevine operated well and everyone in the organization already knew about David's new position, they all cheered. She watched Nate, who stood by one of the framed paintings of the original Villa. He wore a smile, but she recognized that hard look in his eyes. He was pretending well and even raised his glass to salute David, but she knew her husband. Inwardly, he seethed and it was only a matter of time or a more convenient place before his anger boiled over.

Samuel continued. "Of course, we are also blessed with the development leadership of Nathan Calebian. It is Nathan's work that has helped us grow as the national kingpin of assisted living facilities."

David now saluted Nate, and Abigail was glad Samuel verbally recognized her husband. Maybe that affirmation would help temper a bit of Nate's resentment.

After the announcement, people started to filter away, a few at a time. Abigail offered the last of her brownies to the departing guests, then looked for Ruth. She wanted to spend more time with her, but couldn't locate her. After another turn around the room, she peeked around the corner and saw Ruth sitting in a wing chair. Fatigue lined her face. She stifled a yawn with her graceful hands.

David was deep in a discussion with two of the board members. Abigail inched toward him and tried to get his attention. He looked her way, and she motioned toward

No Visible Scars

Ruth. He looked puzzled, but soon excused himself and crossed the room.

"Did you need something?" he asked.

"I've noticed that Ruth seems tired. Maybe she's had enough celebration. Would you like me to take her back to the Villa?"

"Oh, no. I'll do it. It will give me an excuse to leave. Thanks. I had almost forgotten about Granny Ruth. I'll bet you're right. She's not used to this much noise and this many people in one place."

Abigail nodded and started to walk away, then felt David's hand in her own. "You look lovely tonight."

Embarrassed and surprised, she felt herself blush. "Thank you," she said, then hurried to say good-bye to Ruth.

Within fifteen minutes, the crowd had cleared. Abigail picked up some of the remaining glassware even though she knew the cleaning crew would soon invade the building. By morning, all the remaining hors d'oeuvres and napkins that littered the lobby would be removed.

Nate grabbed an unopened bottle of Chandon and tucked it inside his suit coat. As soon as she picked up her purse and her empty crystal platter, they walked toward the elevator and rode down to the main floor.

Samuel waited for them by the main entrance. "A superb party," he said, his white hair shining in the halogen lights over the entrance.

"Yes," said Nate. "A nice turn out."

"I'd like to thank you, son," Samuel said, sticking out his hand. "You handled everything well, and I'm proud of you. I know this wasn't exactly the scenario you had envisioned."

"Sir?"

"Come now, Nathan. We both know how ambitious you are. One of the qualities that makes you such a great development officer. I'm sure you were disappointed by the board's decision."

Abigail tried to move away from the two men, feeling like an intruder. But Samuel smiled at her, and she knew he didn't mind her presence. Nate, on the other hand, seemed more tense than before. His left hand played with the lapel of his suit. Maybe Samuel shouldn't have brought up the subject.

To his credit, Nate played his role well. "I'm sure Dave will do a fine job leading the company."

"Yes, he will," agreed Samuel. "And you will continue to provide leadership to the marketing teams and take us to even greater prosperity. Your composure tonight did not go unnoticed."

"Thank you, sir. Anything for the company."

Samuel took Abigail's hand and kissed it. "And to you as always, a great thank you for the brownies. You know how to cheer this old man with a tasty treat."

She smiled. "My pleasure, sir."

They walked Samuel to his car, then waved good-bye as he slowly maneuvered out of the parking lot and into traffic. "Humpf," said Nate as he grabbed Abigail's elbow and steered her toward their car. "That went better than I thought it would. Maybe if I work extra hard, develop a few more facilities and bring in a greater profit, they'll give me another promotion. Who knows? Dave might grow tired of the whole CEO thing. He'd rather play his guitar anyway."

The lights of the city reflected on the car's hood as they drove home. Abigail sat quietly, reveling in the evening and the compliments she had received about her appearance. She thought of Ruth and hoped she slept well tonight.

At home, she slipped out of her new top, hung it in the closet and snuggled under the sheets. She felt proud of herself for taking the first step with Nate, declaring what she wanted to wear. Maybe next week, she would move the beautiful dress and the wig home and take another step forward. She would definitely have something good to share with the ladies at the next Life Limits meeting.

No Visible Scars

CHAPTER NINETEEN

They passed around the bowl of Hershey's kisses. Each woman took a piece while Cassie filled her palm. Abigail smiled at her friend and gently touched the baby bump that now gave Cassie her signature shape.

Jubilee finished her piece of chocolate and tossed the wrapper into the trash. "Who has something wonderful to share? Who set a boundary this week?"

Abigail raised her hand, catching her watch on the purple scarf entwined around her neck. Before every meeting, she carefully retrieved the scarf from Jubilee's office and wore it proudly.

She fiddled with the scarf and finally freed it from the link on her watch band. "My good news," she said, "is that I set a boundary with my husband. We had a big celebration at work, and I decided to wear my new tank top. This peacock blue one."

She pulled up the picture on her cell phone and passed it around the group. Ooh's and ah's followed as the picture moved from woman to woman. "Best color ever," mumbled Cassie, her mouth full of Hershey kisses.

"How did you set your boundary?" Jubilee prodded.

"I sort of manipulated my husband." She smiled as she remembered. "I told him that by wearing something festive, the VIP's at the party would think he agreed with the reason for the celebration. It's kind of a long story, and I don't want to go into all of it, but I felt as if I finally beat my husband at his own game."

"Hurray!" shouted Martha.

But Jubilee frowned. "Abigail, I do applaud your courage to step up and state something you've wanted for a long time. But our purpose in setting boundaries is not revenge, manipulation or any type of reverse abuse."

"Abuse?" said Cassie. "How can you call that abuse after everything he's done to Abigail? That's not fair."

Jubilee continued. "Setting boundaries is the best way to protect our hearts and sometimes, we end up protecting our very lives. But we don't do it at the expense of someone else. The best boundary-setting is done through honest confrontation and a mutual agreement on the rules.

"With emotional boundaries, it's a little more difficult. I can understand your confusion, Abigail. It's easy to grow frustrated about how to respond when we finally find the courage to confront others. We have to be careful we don't add to the problem by becoming cruel or bitter."

"So what should Abigail have done?" asked Martha. "How can we learn from this?"

"First, we remind ourselves to respect others, even the person who has stepped over the line. By respecting others, we allow them the right to make their own mistakes yet suffer the consequences. We don't try to fix others, and we are not responsible for how others think or act. We are only responsible for ourselves. Let me ask you, Abigail. Did you feel completely right about manipulating your husband into this acceptance of your boundary? Were you really proud of yourself?"

Proud of herself. She thought about the lies she had told throughout the last months and how she convinced Nate that Life Limits Class was a Bible study, then a crafts class. No, not proud moments. "I hadn't really thought about it until now. Probably on some level, I lowered myself to his tactics and responded as he would have. I played his game, even though I *was* proud of myself for trying to set a boundary."

"Yes," Jubilee nodded. "And we are proud of you as well. But we also want you to keep growing as a human being without becoming a woman who takes advantage of others. We want you to set your boundaries in a way that is respectful and honest so that at the end of the day, you can sleep well, knowing your heart is pure."

Cassie shook her head. "But isn't there a delicate line here? Maybe N...uhm...Abigail's husband only understands a boundary when it's on his level, sneaky and manipulative. If she had been completely honest with him, he probably wouldn't have responded in the same way. She'd still be hiding behind her desire to show courage."

Cassie had a point. If she had been completely honest with Nate and told him she wanted to wear the tank top because she was tired of the clothes he chose for her, he would have yelled at her and demanded she change back to her usual beige and boring look. He never would have listened to her speak honestly.

Yet...she hadn't really tried to be honest. She had decided to beat him at his own game and trick him into letting her wear that wonderful color. "I'm confused," she said and reached for another chocolate.

"Hand me a couple more," said Cassie.

Jubilee nodded. "Let me explain it this way. When we begin to set boundaries, we are working against years of habits and patterns of behavior. We may be somewhat at fault for letting those lines blur and sometimes, it is the fault of the other person. Often, it's a relational mistake on the part of both."

"Yeah, I can see that," said Lydia, patting her gray hair. "I've let my kids run over me for years and now it's hard to say, 'Enough.'"

"Exactly," said Jubilee. "But in time, as we work through the issues, we set new rules of behavior. At first, we will meet with resistance. Anger is often the first response."

Jubilee had that right. Abigail had seen enough of Nate's anger to last her a lifetime.

"When we are faced with that anger, it helps to just walk out of the room. Put distance between you and the other person. Refuse to be his target. Sometimes, you'll need to speak and say respectfully, 'I don't appreciate your tone. Can we both take a minute before we proceed?'"

Like that would work. Nate's impulse was to scream obscenities, break something, grab her hair or toss her onto the bed. She almost laughed out loud at the idea of asking him to "Take a minute."

But Jubilee continued. "Ladies, I am not advocating that you remain in the same room with a person who is violent. Any type of physical action against you is cause for a call to 9-1-1 or at least, for you to get in your car and drive away. You cannot talk sensibly to a person who is throwing something at you or brandishing a knife."

Abigail shivered. At least she had never faced a knife. Nate had never cut her or threatened her with a gun. He had never hit her, although he had left plenty of bruises from grabbing her wrists or twisting fingers. She massaged her cock-eyed pinky finger.

"Are we clear about the physical boundaries?" Jubilee asked.

Everyone nodded. Jubilee passed a basket for whoever wanted to contribute to the fund against domestic violence. Abigail threw in her last ten.

"All right. We're clear on that subject. Remember those who break boundaries are basically working from a mindset of control. Once they sense they are losing control, they may respond with anger or possibly fear. So we need to counter those powerful emotions with respect and honesty. Let them know we're taking care of ourselves and not attacking them. Does that help your confusion, Abigail?"

"A bit. Thank you. I'm just not sure that being totally honest with my husband is going to help. I don't think he'll listen, and I think our relationship might get worse if I try."

Jubilee seemed sad. "You may be correct, and if the situation grows worse, you must protect yourself. But by remaining honest, respectful and courageous, you can teach your husband how to respect you. The best relationships are built on mutual respect, and honest communication is the key."

Cassie squeezed Abigail's hand. "Well, I for one have learned something tonight. This boundaries business isn't easy, but I'm still proud of my friend for trying."

"Absolutely," said Jubilee. "We all continue to learn, not only about boundaries but even more about ourselves, about who we are and how to embrace our true identities, about what we want in life and how we can live in relationship with others. We need other people, but often that means dealing with the mess, finding ways to compromise and meet each other halfway."

The rest of the meeting was spent discussing the last session, scheduled for the following week. Everyone decided to bring a special treat. Abigail offered her brownies.

"The best you've ever tasted," said Cassie.

〰〰〰

On the way home Abigail swiped at tears. "I don't know what I'll do without that group of women. I've enjoyed them so much, and I really need to learn more."

"So why stop now?" asked Cassie as she swerved to avoid an armadillo in the road. "Dumb animal," she said. "Why do they always come out at night and play dodge the cars?"

"What do you mean, 'Why stop now?'"

"Nate already knows you're gone every Wednesday night to our so-called pretend crafts class. Why not just continue to meet with Jubilee? Maybe you could do some counseling with her. You know, one-on-one stuff."

"That's a great idea."

"Of course. I'm the queen of great ideas."

Abigail took a deep breath. "But how do I respect Nate and tell him honestly about my need for counseling? Like Jubilee said tonight, 'Be honest and communicate with respect.' She doesn't even know we've been lying...*I've been lying about going to a crafts class.*"

"I don't know. You'll figure it out. I'm proud of you for the progress you've made, girlfriend. Not that I'm perfect either. I've had to set a boundary with Rick, too."

"You have? I thought you two had the perfect relationship."

Cassie snorted. "Are you kidding? There is no such thing, although I must say Rick is nearly perfect in every way. Have you ever seen my man in swim trunks? My, oh my."

Abigail giggled. "So how did you set a boundary with Mister Perfect?"

"I reminded him about Smart Art, my dream studio. He's been so busy with his business, he's forgotten to help me look for a place so we can sign the lease and move forward. I had to nudge him to set a deadline for the launch of my new career."

"Really? And what is that date?"

"Three months after the baby comes. We figure by that time, our wonderful child will be sleeping through the night and I'll be able to devote time to the studio. Plus, I'll put the baby in a play pen while I set everything up in the store. You know, having a baby on the premises is good for business. People are attracted to them."

"That sounds wonderful. I can hardly wait to celebrate with you."

"You'll be invited to the launch of Smart Art, of course. Wear your blue dress."

Abigail sighed. "Maybe by that time, I'll know how to be honest and respectful with Nate although I don't have much hope for his response."

Cassie parked in front of Abigail's house and reached over to take her hand. "Remember what Jubilee said. If you ever get into real trouble with Nate, call 9-1-1. And then call me. Rick and I will come running with some type of weapon."

"Really? Do you have a gun?"

"No, but we can be pretty fierce with rakes and hoes. And I have a baseball bat."

Abigail laughed at the visual of Cassie storming into her house with a rake in her hands. The thought of having to call 9-1-1 and report her husband seemed so far-fetched, she couldn't imagine it. "Let's hope that scenario never takes place."

"Yeah. Let's hope. Good night, friend."

She walked slowly to the front door. She could hear Nate's music playing through the speaker system that reverberated throughout the house. The lyrics of "Here Comes Goodbye" reminded her how Nate often played sad songs about relationships that went sour, of lost loves and depressing endings.

As she slipped inside, she saw him asleep in his recliner, an empty wine glass on the table next to him. She quietly set the house alarm and tiptoed upstairs. Better to take off her makeup and slip into bed without waking him.

After she finished in the bathroom, she decided to take another look at her beautiful peacock blue tank top, to imagine wearing it to Cassie's launch of Smart Art. But when she turned on the light in her walk-in closet, she gasped.

On the floor, in tattered shreds lay the shiny remains of her precious tank top. Lying on top was a note. "Wear what I tell you to wear. You're my wife. Submit."

She fell to her knees and choked on sobs of despair. What good were boundaries if they didn't work?

No Visible Scars

CHAPTER TWENTY

Abigail carried another plateful of brownies into the Villa and handed them to the receptionist at the front desk. "Be sure everybody on staff gets one," she said. "I'll be in the corner suite with Ruth."

"Sure, honey, and thanks," said the woman.

As she walked down the hallway, she noticed new decorations at the residents' doorways. A teddy bear with a pink bow around his neck sat on a tiny high chair. The photograph of a Labrador retriever, staring at a lake with ducks swimming across its shiny surface. In front of Ruth's door, a brass treble clef sign, surrounded by baby's breath and a scarlet ribbon which held a yellow rose.

She lightly tapped on the door, then turned the doorknob when she heard the sweet reply of "Come in, please."

Ruth stood in front of her stove, pushing the button that sent heat underneath her tea kettle. "Oh, my dear," she said. "You're just in time for hibiscus delight, a new tea I want to try. Did you bring your wonderful treats with you again?"

"I did," said Abigail as she pulled a small Tupperware container out of her bag. She opened the lid and the smell of her specialty chocolate drifted from the brownies inside.

"Have you had a good week?" Ruth asked as she handed Abigail a floral napkin.

For a moment, she thought about telling Ruth everything that had happened. Ruth would understand how important that peacock blue tank top had been and how devastated she was to find it tattered, lying like a dead bird on her closet floor. But Ruth was, after all, David's great grandmother. Abigail didn't want to spill any family secrets that might damage the integrity of the company. She also didn't want to worry Ruth about something she could not fix.

No, it was her own problem. Only *she* owned the responsibility to do something about it. If she only knew what that something was.

She wanted to tell Ruth how she had dressed this morning, how she had kept one piece of the shredded tank top and carefully pinned it to the underside of her bra. Next to her heart. Nate might have destroyed something beautiful, but he could not take more of her soul than she would give him. She would wear that tiny sliver of cloth to remind herself she *did* count for something. Someday, somehow, she would find the courage to tell Nate exactly what she thought of his behavior. But none of this could be shared with Ruth.

"It was a busy week," Abigail admitted. She bit into one of her brownies, tried to take comfort in the chocolately sweetness. She watched as Ruth carefully poured the crimson-colored tea into first Abigail's cup and then her own.

Ruth moved gracefully around her kitchenette, replacing the tea kettle on her stove and cleaning up a bit of water that spilled. Her orange and red caftan swirled with each movement.

"Did you enjoy the party," Abigail asked, "the celebration of David's promotion?"

Ruth smiled and a glow came over her face. "Oh, my dear, I was so pleased when David asked me to accompany him. I couldn't have been prouder, and of course, the corporate office looks lovely. Your doing, I'm sure."

"Oh, no. We hire designers to come in and make everything beautiful as well as functional. All I did for the party was to bake my brownies."

Ruth took a small bite. "And you do that so well, my dear."

Abigail's throat felt raw with unshed tears. It was so seldom that anyone complimented her, except for Samuel and David. But she wanted more. She wanted to be known for the work she did for the company and ultimately, for her unique identity. No matter what happened in her messed-up life, she wanted to pursue the desire of her heart. She was more certain than ever that she wanted to become a teacher, and she decided to let Ruth in on that little secret.

"Did you ever want to work somewhere besides your home? Did you have a secret ambition, something you wanted to accomplish that seemed like a dream but you wondered how to make it happen? Something that kept gnawing at your soul until you finally had the courage to do something about it?" She had probably said too much, but once she started sharing with Ruth, she couldn't stop.

"I mean, you know, I've wanted to do this one thing forever. Ever since I was a little girl, I've wanted to be a school teacher. I started college with a major in education and I enjoyed my classes. I worked hard and made good grades, but then...."

"Then what?" Ruth quiet voice spurred her on.

"Then I met Nate and he wined and dined me. I fell in love with him and he proposed and I married him. Now I work for him." She wrung her hands and inhaled deeply. "He wants me at the office, always available. I've never returned to my original dream. I've never been able to actually *be* who I want to be, and it's about to kill me.

"Sometimes I dream about it at night. I'm helping children learn how to read or how to add simple problems. We're having such a fun time together." A half-giggle escaped, followed by a sigh. "Then I wake up and I'm just plain old me, working in an office job with no hope of ever being with those children. I just want to cry."

Ruth's eyes filled with empathetic tears. "But my dear, you must do something about this. Becoming a teacher is an honorable vocation. Surely you can take a few classes, work at earning your degree a little at a time. One of my grandsons...hmm...or is it a great grandson? You know, there are so many, sometimes I forget what the proper generation is. Anyway, he earned his degree by doing everything on the computer. Couldn't you do something like that?"

Abigail sighed and tore off another bite of her brownie. "I wish it were that simple."

"But why isn't it possible? What is keeping you from moving toward your goal, this dream you have of becoming an instructor? I think you would make a splendid teacher."

She hated to say anything more. She was not going to tell Ruth about her relationship with Nate.

Ruth had a faraway look in her eyes. "When I was a young woman, I thought life with my first husband would be wonderful. We had so many dreams, so many hopes. But he died young, and I was left with no children. My mother-in-law, Naomi, and I clung to each other. I moved in with her and we grieved together.

"But even in the midst of her intense grief, I saw Naomi had something I didn't—an extraordinary fortitude. She was determined to make life better for us. She, too, was a recent widow. Even though we both reeled from the loss of our husbands and she for her son, she accepted the challenge. She helped me understand how God really cared for two bereaved women. Together, we survived. She was my friend, my mentor and my companion through the darkest of days. My precious Naomi."

Ruth sighed and patted Abigail's hand. "I've told you my story to remind you that we women are made of strong stuff. Naomi and I met the challenge and found a better life. You, my dear, can do the same. I believe in you."

Abigail's eyes filled with tears of gratitude. She replied huskily, "Thank you for your confidence in me.. I will try. I'll make you proud of me."

"Oh, my dear, you miss the point. You must learn to be proud of yourself, to fight for your dream because it is yours. The peace of your soul is dependent on your becoming the woman God created you to be."

Be proud of herself and fight for her dream. Become the woman God created her to be. "That sounds like the same advice I'm learning in my Life Limits Class. Thank you for reminding me of what I need to do."

Ruth stifled a yawn. "Oh, my dear, I am so sorry, but I do believe I need a little nap."

Abigail stood and carried her tea cup to the kitchenette. She leaned over to hug Ruth good-bye. But Ruth called to her before she stepped out the door. "I wonder, my dear, if you might check on something for me."

"Of course. Anything you need."

"One of my friends, Lou Ann, has always thrived in the painting class. She makes the most beautiful watercolors. But lately, she hasn't been able to work on her art, because an additional price has been charged for the classes, beyond her budget. It seems odd to me, this sudden increase in the charges, and I promised Lou Ann I would ask someone in authority. But I forgot to mention it to David, and he's so very busy these days. Is that something you can look into?"

"Yes. I'll ask the director of this Villa and possibly, my husband. We'll find out who is charging this extra amount and why."

"Thank you, my dear. Now, I really must lie down. Thank you for the wonderful brownies. I hope to see you again soon."

Abigail quietly exited Ruth's room, then hurried to the director's office. She rounded the corner and found Melissa finishing one of her brownies, then slurping from her coffee cup. Melissa seemed a bit embarrassed, but Abigail smiled. "I'm glad you like them."

"Best ever." Melissa wiped her mouth with a napkin, then reached into her top drawer and pulled out her lip gloss. "How can I help you?" she asked, as she opened the tube and carefully applied it to her lips. She motioned toward the chair in front of her desk, and Abigail sat down.

"I've been visiting with Ruth."

"Lovely woman. Did you know she's 95? It's amazing she still lives so independently."

"Yes. We love having tea together. But Ruth is concerned about something, and I thought I'd ask you about it."

"Oh? What's the problem?"

"It seems one of her friends loves to paint, a resident named Lou Ann. Recently, an extra charge has been applied to the painting class and she can't afford it anymore. Is that true? I know sometimes residents become confused or believe something is true when it's only a miscommunication. Or they might dream something, then believe it actually happened. Do you think that's the case with Lou Ann?"

Melissa nodded and reached for her reading glasses. "We've been told to charge extra fees for any additional activities: art classes, Bible studies, even when we shuttle residents to another location for movies or theatre productions. It isn't a large increase in the charges, but it can add up. I'm sorry Lou Ann is upset about it, but my hands are tied."

No Visible Scars

Abigail was puzzled. "But who authorized these changes? Usually I'm the one who types up memos and faxes them to all the Villas. But I've never seen any information about additional charges."

Melissa opened a file drawer. "Let me see. I think I have the latest memo right here." She shuffled through some papers. "Yes. Here it is." She pulled a page from the pile and handed it to Abigail. "You can read it for yourself. It's dated a couple of months ago, but the changes were effective the first of this month."

Abigail knew the letterhead well and the tagline that scrolled across the top of the page, "Villas de Comfort—The Best Place for Senior Living."

She read the memo out loud, "'Effective June 1, new charges will be assessed on each resident's account for extra activities. These activities include: classes of any kind, activities outside the Villas, Bible studies, choirs, et cetera. Please make notations in each resident's file so families may be invoiced properly. Although we regret these surcharges, the increased cost of gas for the shuttle and liability insurance makes this decision necessary.'" The letter contained the standard signature line, Villas de Comfort, Corporate Office, Kansas City, MO.

Abigail shook her head. "I knew nothing about this."

Melissa nodded. "Some of my staff are pretty fired up about it. It's a hassle to have to record every time one of the residents goes anywhere or wants to do something extra. And we haven't even begun to hear complaints from the families."

"But the corporate office likes to enlist opinions from the families on any changes."

Melissa shook her head and took off her reading glasses. "Obviously, that policy slipped through the cracks in this instance. Look, I don't want to be the one to complain, but since you work at Corporate, maybe you can do something. We don't want a bunch of unhappy residents on our hands. You can imagine the collateral damage."

"Yes. May I have a copy of this letter?"

Melissa turned around, placed the letter on the three-in-one printer and punched the copy button. The whir of the machine filled the room.

Abigail reached for the copy. "Thank you, Melissa, for being candid with me."

"I like my job. I want to keep it."

"Of course. There's no danger of that changing because you showed me this memo."

"Just so we're clear about it." Melissa glanced at her watch. "I have a staff meeting in a few. Do you need anything else?"

"No. Thank you. I'll just pick up my plate from the staff break room, if the brownies are all gone."

"Oh, I'm sure they are."

As she drove home, Abigail thought about the memo. She had no real power in the company, so there was nothing she could do about it, except ask Nate. After what he had done to her beautiful top, she didn't want to talk to him about anything—ever again.

Still, she had promised Melissa and Ruth she would check on this issue and find out what was happening. The question was, how?

On Monday, Abigail ate lunch at her desk. Nate and David drove to Longhorn Steakhouse for lunch with Samuel, a strategy session to help the Villas branch out into another state. They wanted to move farther east into Indiana, Ohio and Pennsylvania, but one of their top competitors already operated with a solid hold in Pittsburgh.

"We're plotting it out," Nate told her that morning. "Looking for ways to beat out the competition."

Abigail knew she had only one hour to search for answers to Lou Ann's dilemma. She called Teresa at the Iowa City Villa, an efficient manager and a skilled communicator. Teresa's motto was credibility. She would tell the truth.

After a few greetings, Abigail said, "You're such a good manager. No wonder your employees always mark you high on the annual evaluations."

"Cut to the chase, Abigail. You don't call me that often. Something must be up at Corporate."

She smiled and thought of Jubilee, who would love Teresa's authenticity. "I won't keep you long, but I *am* puzzled about something. I wondered if you could help me without letting anyone else know I called."

"Got it. What's the problem?"

"One of our local Villas in the KC Metro received a memo about extra charges for residents' activities: art classes, shuttle transportation, book clubs, that sort of thing. Did you receive that memo as well?"

"Sure did, and I can tell you some of our residents are mighty upset about it. You know, these folks and their families keep track of every penny. Anything added to their bill becomes worrisome."

"I'm sorry about that. Do you remember when that new policy went into effect?"

"Sure do, because I thought it was kind of ironic."

"Ironic? How do you mean?" Abigail messed with the cuticle on her thumbnail.

"Our memo was effective April first. April Fool's Day. I thought it was some sort of joke. Then I realized, the joke is on Corporate. If we get too many complaints and residents start leaving for a different facility, the Villas will lose money. So that's the irony. They think they're making a little here and there, but in the end—they might lose much more. The odd thing is that it isn't really that much."

"You mean it doesn't add up to much money?"

"Right. By the time you figure a little extra added to a few activities, Corporate isn't going to get rich in Iowa. Between you and me, it feels like someone's padding his or her pocket."

"Oh, dear. I'm sure that can't be happening. This must be a huge mistake, but thank you for being candid with me."

"Yeah. You can count on me."

She thought about the other branches in Illinois, Nebraska, Missouri, Colorado and Michigan. If these additional charges were happening there as well, then those small amounts would start adding up.

"One more thing, Teresa. Have you talked to any of the directors at other facilities? Has this memo gone into effect across the board? Or is it just here in the Metro and at your location in Iowa?"

"Oh, it's everywhere. We directors operate a massive grapevine and keep in touch through emails and text. Nebraska got the memo in March and Colorado in May. Ours in April. Looks like a different month for each state. But let me be clear, Abigail. We're all devoted to our jobs and to our residents. Even if we disagree with Corporate on this, we're not going to mutiny or anything. We're loyal to the Villas de Comfort."

"Thank you. I appreciate that."

"So…can you do anything about this? Or is it a done deal?"

"I don't know. I'll check it out and…I'd appreciate if this conversation between us went no further. Confidentiality is vital."

"What conversation?" She heard the grin in Teresa's voice.

"Right. Have a great day."

Stunned, Abigail clicked her gel pen again and again. Surely Nate wasn't padding his pockets. David would never stand for any type of questionable integrity. Neither would Samuel and the board of directors. Unless of course, one of them had decided to step over the line.

If she pressed forward to investigate further, Nate would be angry. After the incident with her tank top, she shuddered to think what he might destroy this time. Good thing her beautiful dress was safe with Cassie. Just when she wanted to ask him again about becoming a teacher. Now she needed to confront him about this memo.

It didn't make sense. Nate had plenty of money, stocks and bonds, a portfolio any executive would be proud of. He didn't need extra funds. What was the point? Unless this was his revenge against the board of directors for refusing to promote him to CEO.

She rubbed her temples, tried to chase back the beginnings of a headache. This was too much to figure out during one lunch hour. Nate and David would return soon. She opened her salad container, then reached into her top drawer for some Ibuprofen. She didn't have to take any action right away. She would think about it for a few days.

She reached inside the hidden pouch and pulled out the picture of herself in the dress. Freedom and strength. She ached to resurrect the happy Abigail in the picture, to be more resilient than her fear. She folded the picture and hid it again. If only she had the courage to buy a beautiful frame and slip that picture inside. To place that photo right smack in the middle of Nate's desk.

Or wear her dress in public. Why couldn't she take another confident step forward? Not to push the boundary entirely with Nate, at least not yet. But to help herself feel more empowered.

She texted Cassie. "Will pick up my dress after work. Wearing it tomorrow when I visit Ruth."

She finished her salad as the elevator dinged and she heard Nate's voice. "If we can land that Pennsylvania account, Dave, that would be the icing on the cake."

Nate and David walked into the main reception area together. David nodded at Abigail while Nate ignored her.

"So what's the next step?" Nate pressed. "Do I fly east next week?"

"I think that's a good idea," said David, as both of them moved down the hallway. "Book a flight and check out the investor Samuel knows in Philly. Maybe he can get us started with more networking in the east."

"Right. Strike while the iron is hot. Abby!" Nate hollered from around the corner. "Get me on a flight to Philadelphia. First Class. I can't stand those snotty little kids in coach."

"Right away," she said as she clicked on her bookmarked file for the airlines and started the reservation process. Relief flowed through her. With Nate gone for a couple of days, scoping out potential territory and meeting with investors, she would have time for more research, to figure out what to do about this situation.

The interoffice page sounded. Nate's office. She punched the button. "Yes sir?"

"Did you get my flight?"

"I'm just confirming it now and printing out your boarding pass. You leave next Tuesday morning at eight. It's a direct flight, and Enterprise will have a rental car waiting for you."

"Good. Make sure it's a Caddie. The first impression with investors has to be perfect."

"Yes. I remember how upset you were the last time you traveled and didn't get a full-sized car." Upset seemed too mild an adjective. Furious was a better word. He had screamed at her all the way from the airport to home just because he felt crunched inside a small convertible. As if she could control everything that happened when he was on the road.

The interoffice page clicked off. No thank you from Nate. No affirmation that she had done a good job and he was pleased with her.

She was only the executive assistant who obeyed every order and hated every minute of it. More than ever, she wanted to leave her job, escape to a quiet little campus and become a teacher. To live alone, free of Nate and his controlling expectations.

Ridiculous. That would mean a divorce or a separation at the very least. She didn't want to end her marriage and live without any security, worry about paying the bills like Mama. But she hated feeling trapped inside this corporate zoo with her angry husband.

Maybe if she cooked him a special meal tonight, she could casually ask him about the memo. No. It would make more sense to secretly search his files. Next week when he was gone. All she needed to do until Nate boarded that plane was avoid making him angry. Don't let him suspect she was searching for clues.

Jubilee would caution against any type of manipulation. But this was an unfair edict against the residents and possibly a blight on the company. For the sake of Ruth, the residents and all the others in the company, she must do everything possible to find out the truth.

Another headache pounded. Her temples throbbed as she rubbed her neck. She wished Nate would let her get a full body massage, but she had asked once and he refused. Some complaint about a stranger's hands on his woman's body.

She decided to concentrate on the positives and pulled off a turquoise Post-it-note to make a list:

Think happy thoughts.
Cassie and the baby.
Smart Art.
Sunshine.
Be an authentic woman. Who am I?
Make it through today. Only four more hours.
Finish any paperwork Nate needs to take with him.
Survive the night.
Decide what to do about the problem…later.

CHAPTER TWENTY-ONE

The next Monday, Abigail left the office early to visit Ruth. Everything Nate needed for his next trip was already filed and stacked on his desk. His clothes laundered at home. His ticket and boarding pass tucked into his briefcase.

She would have one glorious hour with Ruth and surprise her by wearing something besides her usual bland office clothes. Cassie had cheered for her when she picked up the dress. "You go, girl!"

She retrieved the Von Maur sack from her trunk and hurried into the public restroom at the Villa. From the moment she slipped the dress over her head, she felt like a new woman. Such a beautiful mixture of blues, the sheen of the fabric, the joy of looking at herself in the mirror. Her eyes sparkled with excitement. Her pulse quickened.

She stepped into the hallway, greeted several staff members and stopped to shake the hand of a gentleman in his walker. "Pretty lady," he said with a wink.

"Thank you for noticing me. You made my day."

She imagined Ruth's reaction would be one of sheer delight. She would gush about the colors and want to feel the fabric. She would encourage Abigail to wear more of the same.

Someday, she would also wear her wig and surprise Ruth. One step at a time, and one boundary at a time with Nate.

She turned into the hallway and headed toward the corner suite. But as she passed the water fountain, she saw Nate standing at the nurses' station.

What was he doing here? She looked around for a place to hide.

Too late. He turned and saw her. A look of disbelief on his face, he marched toward her.

This was it. Her watershed moment, as Jubilee would say. Her heart thundered, but she squared her shoulders and prepared for battle. Time to set another boundary and fight for her rights. Make Ruth proud of her. Put into practice everything she had learned. She had the advantage of surprise and of being in a public place. Nate would not make a scene at a Villa.

He grabbed her arm and squeezed hard. "What are you doing in that get up?"

"It's my dress, Nate. It was a gift from some of my friends. Let go of my arm."

He released her, but bent low. With a hard whisper, he said, "You do not have my permission to wear something like that. We'll settle this at home."

She stepped away from him and spoke a little louder. "No. We'll settle it right here. I'm a grown woman. I have every right to wear what I want." Couldn't he understand how wonderful this dress made her feel? "Look, Nate," she said in a softer tone. "Don't you think it's pretty? And it makes me *feel* pretty." She turned to the side and swished back and forth. "Don't you like the colors?"

He clenched his fists. "No. You need to look like a professional at all times, like our executive assistant should look."

"I know it's important to look professional at my job, but I'm not in the office right now."

One of the nurses moved down the hallway with a tray full of medicines. She gave Nate a sideways glance.

He grabbed Abigail's hand. "Let's go outside. Don't embarrass both of us in front of the staff."

Outside the building, Abigail moved away from him. She stayed close to the entrance, in case she needed to go inside for support. But she intended to state her case.

He paced up and down the sidewalk. "I leave my office and drive over here to check on a director's concern with a nurse and find my wife parading down the hallway in this outfit." He pointed at the dress, a sneer on his face.

"Outfit? This beautiful dress? You have no idea what a wonderful gift this was…how it makes me feel every time I put it on."

"Every time? Where else are you wearing it? What kind of secret life are you hiding from me?"

She rolled her eyes. "Get real, Nate. It's no secret life. Sometimes I wear the dress when Cassie and I go shopping. That's all." She moved a bit closer. "Can't we agree on a compromise? You're always talking about effective compromises in business. What if I continue to wear professional dress at the office, but I choose what to wear outside the office...when I'm with my friends or at church."

"At church? Absolutely not. In fact, I'm going to call Pastor Dennis and tell him you're not behaving like a submissive wife."

She wanted to laugh. "Really? Do you know how ridiculous you sound? By the way, when you call the pastor, ask him if his wife gets to choose her clothes." She crossed her arms.

He started to say something, but she held up her hand. "Hear me out, Nate. I want to be honest about my feelings." She took a deep breath. "You have no idea how much you've hurt me, because the damage is hidden inside. The emotional woundings, like a knife slashing through my heart and leaving my soul bleeding in tiny pieces, stealing every bit of my self-worth."

She paced back and forth in front of the entrance. "It's kind of like one of those kids' toys. You know the colorful pegs you hit with a mallet until all the pegs are pounded down? That's what you've done to me. You've pounded away at me until I'm so far down the hole, I can't see my way out. Do you understand what you've done to me?"

A family walked toward the entrance of the Villa. Nate greeted them with his business-as-usual smile. When the door closed behind them, he turned toward Abigail. "You're acting like a hysterical woman, and I haven't done anything wrong. I pay for everything you have and provide the very best for both of us."

He shook his head. "But I get your point about a compromise. All right. You can wear this dress when you visit the Villas or when you're with Cass. But not at church. And definitely not at work. Deal?"

She thought for a moment. "It's a step forward. Okay. Deal. For now."

"What do you mean 'for now'?" His face started to redden.

She swallowed hard. Breathed deeply. Time to make sure this boundary would stand. "I mean if you destroy this dress, I will drive to Von Maur and buy another one just like it. Maybe two more. And I will use your credit card to do it." She turned away, her dress swishing with the sudden movement. "See you at home."

She glanced at her watch. Ruth would be ready for her nap soon. A visit was impossible now. She marched toward her car, opened the door and slid into the front seat. She looked back at Nate. His mouth was open, his hands balled into fists.

She drove away slowly, then remembered her office clothes in the Villa's restroom. Who cared? She had plenty of ugly clothes at home.

❧❧❧

As she grated cheese, she wondered who would show up tonight. If it was the angry Nate, she was prepared to call Cassie and stay at her house for a while. If it was the businessman, she was ready to talk more about compromise.

She stirred his favorite Mexican casserole. Might as well try to meet him halfway. Maybe turn the argument into a real discussion. Agree to disagree but give each other space. If their marriage could only work like a partnership. For that to happen, Nate would have to change and she would have to become more hopeful.

Probably not possible. Jubilee taught them how setting healthy limits could work out, but only if both sides were willing to address the issues.

She bit into a corn chip. Pursed her lips at the bitter lime seasoning.

The garage door rumbled open as Nate's car entered. The engine turned off. The door into the back entry opened. She expected it to slam shut, but was surprised when it closed softly. His steps in the living room. She felt his presence in the kitchen even before she saw him. Her throat was dry. She reached for a glass of water.

He didn't look at her. Took a wine glass out of the cabinet and poured himself a Merlot.

She decided to make the first move. "Do you want to talk? Or are you hungry?"

"I'm tired," he said. "It's been an exhausting day. Extra responsibilities, a problem with collateral damage at one of the Villas and disappointment with my wife."

"Disappointment?"

"That's right. You have disrespected me and my authority in the home." His finger tapped on the countertop. He pulled open the drawer under the silverware and reached for the scissors.

Her dress was hanging in the closet, separate from the office clothes. Surely he wouldn't call her bluff and cut it up.

"Where's your purse?"

"In the front hallway." She turned off the stove and followed him. "Why? What are you doing?"

She reached for her purse, but he shoved her out of the way. He dumped the contents on the floor, picked up her billfold and pulled out her one credit card. Then he sliced it in half. "I'll give you an allowance every two weeks. You can buy groceries and whatever we need for the house. If you want anything else, you'll have to ask my permission."

He stomped into the kitchen and slammed the scissors back into the drawer.

Breathing hard, she watched him from the doorway. "You're not being fair. This isn't a compromise."

"Shut up! End of discussion." He reached inside his pocket and pulled out a 3x5 card. Set it on the countertop and carried his wine upstairs.

She waited until she heard the sound of the shower, then looked at the card. Printed in Nate's careful lettering, the words of First Peter chapter three: *"Wives, fit in with your husbands' plans. Don't be concerned about the outward beauty that depends on jewelry, or beautiful clothes, or hair arrangement. Be beautiful inside with a gentle and quiet spirit."*

❀❀❀

Abigail barely slept, her mind a whirlwind of anxiety. On the spiritual level, maybe Nate was right. He was after all, a leader in the church, and he certainly knew how to throw scripture at her. She hadn't exactly acted with a gentle and quiet spirit. But was it so wrong to wear her beautiful dress?

On the other hand, she had tried to set another healthy boundary, and it backfired. Maybe she should talk to Jubilee and find out her perspective.

Now she would have even less financial freedom. No credit card. No opportunity to make her own decisions about purchases. Only a cash allowance for groceries every two weeks. Trapped in this emotional prison with an angry husband for a warden.

Might as well get up and start thinking about another day. It was only five o'clock, but a cup of hot tea might settle her. She grabbed her robe and headed downstairs, saw the mess on the floor where Nate dumped her purse. She scooped everything back in and swiped at a tear as the phone rang.

"Abigail?"

David's voice sounded strained.

"Yes. What's wrong?"

"The Villa called. Granny Ruth...died in her sleep. One of the nurses found her."

"Oh, no. Oh, David."

"I know. I can't believe it." A sigh. "Tell Nate I have to make the arrangements. I'll be in late...or I don't know...I probably won't make it in today."

"Of course. Please let us know what we can do to help. Oh, my. I don't know what we'll do without her." A catch in her throat.

"I'll talk to you later...when I know more. 'Bye."

She hung up the phone and sank into the kitchen chair. Her head in her arms, she wept for the loss of her precious friend. Ruth would never see the beautiful blue dress, never share tea with her again. Never know how she had tried to make her dream come true.

No Visible Scars

CHAPTER TWENTY-TWO

As the funeral home director ushered them to their seats, Abigail followed Nate into the cathedral. The room was already half-filled with residents of the Overland Park Villa, staff and people from the community. A good portion of the front seats were reserved for David, his parents, his six brothers and two sisters, plus all the grandchildren and extended family. Colorful sprays of flowers filled the front of the room and extended along the sides. Ruth would have loved the colors, textures and flowing ribbons that accented each bouquet.

Abigail forced herself to look at the casket at the front of the chapel. It was a beautiful peacock blue color. A large spray of yellow roses covered the top and draped down the sides.

Earlier in the week, she visited the funeral home and spent moments alone with Ruth's body. It helped to have some time alone, to grieve for the loss of this incredible woman who became a mentor in such a short amount of time.

Abigail stood before the open casket and stared at the beautiful gold lame' outfit Ruth wore, accessorized with a brilliant yellow scarf around her neck. Gold bangles set on her wrists while her white hair fanned out on the pillow. She seemed so young and vibrant, even in death. Her skin fairly smooth under the makeup although the age spots on her hands told the truth about her years.

You probably have no idea how much I loved you, Ruth, even though I hope you somehow felt it. You showed me how to be a gracious yet strong woman. Your beauty was exceeded only by your poise and strength. I so enjoyed our tea times together and how you set your own boundaries. You knew when you were tired and needed to rest. You weren't afraid to ask me to leave. Even those statements taught me how to set my own life limits. Thank you for sharing your heart with me and teaching me how to be a woman of character.

A cellist sat on the stage, softly playing through Clair de Lune, the Canon in D and then the Moonlight Sonata. Sunbeams shafted through the stained glass windows and formed a halo on the casket. Abigail pulled a tissue from her black clutch and wiped a tear. Nate hated it when she cried and looked a mess for hours. He told her she was "an ugly crier," so she tried to keep tears stuffed inside her soul. But today, right now, they threatened near the surface.

Nate put his arm around her and pulled her close. She flinched, wondering why he chose this moment to show affection. Maybe he wanted to impress Samuel and the members of the board, seated directly behind. Or maybe he felt some sympathy although she doubted he would ever understand her feelings for Ruth.

No matter. The façade of affection didn't last more than a few minutes. He soon pulled away and fiddled with his cell phone, answered a few emails then set his phone on mute. He leaned over as she wiped another tear and whispered, "Don't make a scene."

The family started to file in and quickly filled all the reserved seats in the front. David carried his guitar and joined the pastor on the stage. The cellist finished Moonlight Sonata, then waited as David strummed through several chord progressions.

Then he sang alone, a song Abigail had never heard. Perhaps it was composed from one of the poems he wrote. Ruth once shared a scrapbook full of songs David had written and composed into music, but this song seemed filled with poignant meaning.

Abigail had never heard him sing an entire song in full voice. A strong baritone though he clearly grieved. His face etched with fatigue. His chin quivered as he memorialized his great grandmother through the music they both loved.

"You are my light, Lord, and my salvation. Whom shall I fear?

You are my refuge and the stronghold of my life. Of whom shall I be afraid?

One thing have I asked of you, Lord, and that I will seek

That I may dwell in your house, Lord, in your presence, all the days of my life

To behold and gaze upon your beauty, Lord, and your delightful loveliness.

You will hide me in the shelter of your wings as I wait for you."

She felt carried along by the melody as he sang his tribute to Ruth and the God she served. The words and the chords emanated a peace she wanted for herself, a mellow love, the blessing of a loving family.

When he strummed the last chord, he placed his guitar on a stand, then gently touched Ruth's casket before he sat in the second row next to a tow-headed little boy. One of his many nephews, no doubt. The child cuddled close. Abigail hoped David felt some comfort from this little one who obviously loved him.

The entire chapel seemed to sigh as the pastor stood and slowly made his way to the podium. He adjusted his glasses, nodded toward the family, then began to read the obituary.

"Ruth Judah passed from this life and into eternity on Tuesday, June 22, at the Villas de Comfort in Overland Park, Kansas. She was preceded in death by her beloved husband, Beau, and her son, Obadiah, who died serving his country in Vietnam.

"Ruth, who was just two days away from her 96th birthday, spent her life taking care of her family, including her mother-in-law, Naomi, with whom she traveled from New York City to Kansas, after her first husband and her father-in-law both died in an influenza epidemic.

"Ruth will be remembered for her beauty, her courage and her loyalty to family. She is mourned by a host of friends and family including her grandson Jesse and his wife Sarah, their sons and daughters and several great-great grandchildren. The family requests that memorials be sent to the Wounded Warriors program which helps support veterans who have been injured in the line of duty."

Abigail suddenly felt even more bereft. Cassie, of course, was her friend forever, but Abigail already missed how Ruth shared a cup of tea, reminisced about the past and labeled her brownies as "Wonderful!" every single time they met. All she had now was a job she hated, a house she despised and a husband who didn't understand. Nate offered nothing but pain and confusion.

As the pastor spoke the closing prayer, she bowed her head and whispered, "Dear Ruth, tell God I need help."

Maybe Ruth would hear her prayer and remind God that a woman on earth felt all alone in the tragic grief of her difficult marriage. Maybe Ruth would nudge God to rescue her from this sad shadow of a life.

At the cemetery, David and the other great grandsons lifted Ruth's casket from the hearse and carefully carried it to the gravesite. An aging Jesse and Sarah sat near the mound of earth that would soon cover up beautiful Ruth and her earthly body. Abigail stood next to Nate under the cover of the awning.

Once again, David strummed his guitar. "Please sing along with me one of Granny Ruth's favorite songs, 'Amazing Grace.'"

Abigail didn't feel like singing. But Nate grabbed her hand, his strong tenor adding a beautiful harmony to David's lead. Others around them joined in. Finally Abigail found the strength to add her own voice to the final verse.

"When we've been there ten thousand years, bright shining as the sun
We've no less days to sing God's praise than when we first begun."

The funeral director shook hands with all the family members, then urged everyone to come forward for final goodbyes. Once again, he opened the casket so everyone could have a final look at Ruth. Abigail hung back. She felt she had enough grief to last a lifetime, but Nate moved forward to shake hands with Jesse. David finally relaxed his composure as Nate approached him. His shoulders shook as Nate embraced him. Abigail wondered how these two friends could be so different in character yet share the same vision for the Villas.

As they drove away from the cemetery, she looked back at the beautiful casket, shining in the afternoon sun. Standing beside it was David, his head bowed. She knew exactly how he felt. Alone and dreadfully missing the vibrant and wonderful Ruth.

CHAPTER TWENTY-THREE

As she and Cassie entered Hope Gathering, Abigail smelled a tangy barbeque sauce. Maybe someone brought some of those little sausages. She carried her container of brownies while Cassie balanced a bag of chips with her specialty guacamole. Abigail lugged a liter of Diet Coke as well, still wet from the cooler in the back of Cassie's car.

Lydia greeted them at the door. "Come on in, gals. We haven't started eating yet. Jubilee went to the storage room to find some napkins."

The other ladies in the group gathered around Cassie. Missy gingerly touched Cassie's baby bump. "How are you feeling?"

"Pretty good. Just a little indigestion now and then, but I'm starving tonight."

"I brought some queso and Doritos. Looks like we'll have plenty of snacks."

Jubilee hurried into the room with a stack of pastel napkins which she arranged near the paper plates. The dining table was filled with all sorts of wonderful treats. "Ladies," she said. "Is everyone here?" She seemed to count silently as she scanned the room. "I can't tell you how delighted I am that you have successfully completed our Life Limits Class.

Hopefully, it has been helpful. Now, let's party. Who wants to be first in line? Abigail? How about you?"

Abigail touched the place over her heart where she wore the sliver of peacock blue fabric. She smiled at the confidence she felt. "Actually, I think you should be first, Jubilee. You've spent all these weeks teaching us. Let us honor you and let you go first."

The other women clapped. Cassie squeezed Abigail's waist while Jubilee helped herself to the snacks, speared a couple of little sausages with a toothpick, grabbed a handful of chips, then reached for one of Abigail's brownies.

They juggled plates on their laps as they sat around the room in their usual places. Lydia brought Cassie a TV tray for her plate. "Since you don't have much of a lap anymore, gal."

Missy pulled back her long hair, then let it fall again. "I wish I had learned more about setting boundaries when I was younger," she said. "Maybe I wouldn't have made so many foolish decisions."

Jubilee shook her head. "Just the positive feedback, please. All of us have regrets in life, but if we focus on the negatives, we'll have difficulty moving forward. We can't change the past. We can only deal with the present and fill the future with hope."

Missy nodded. "Okay then. I'm glad I've learned how to set boundaries for my health. I'm kicking the smoking habit, a little at a time. I guess I can say, my future is hopeful because one day I'll be a nonsmoker."

"Good for you," said Jubilee as the other women clapped for Missy.

Lydia spoke up. "Well, I'm going to be next, because I'm about to bust. I sat down with my kids and gave them a deadline. They'll be moving out at the end of the summer. Hurray for me! I'm looking forward to my nest finally being empty."

Again, a round of applause.

"Excellent," said Jubilee. "What a wonderful breakthrough! Who's next?"

Amber spoke up. "My kids aren't driving me quite so crazy, although with three of them under the age of five, it's going to be a challenge for a while. But I'm not getting up every five minutes to check on the baby anymore. I let her cry herself to sleep and it only took a couple of nights for her to get the idea. I'm telling you, though, that was hard. I felt like a horrible mother. But my husband and I decided we had to do something. I feel so much better now that I'm getting more sleep."

"I'll have to remember that," said Cassie. "Rick and I are reading lots of parenting books, but talking to those of you who are experienced is probably the best idea. So you let the baby cry? For how long?"

"It's different with every child," said Amber. "My first baby slept through the night at two weeks. It was wonderful. But my second child and this baby don't have the same metabolism. You'll learn the sounds of your baby, what is fear or sickness or just plain stubbornness. I guess the important thing is to not feel guilty about it. Right?" Amber looked at Jubilee who nodded.

"Parenting is difficult on many levels," said Jubilee, "but it's also a joy. After all, these are your bundles of love and the next generation of human beings. Guilt, particularly false guilt, is not a burden we should carry. Enjoy your children but at the same time, don't be afraid to set realistic boundaries. And in the long run, setting those boundaries—those fences to protect our hearts—*will* make parenting more enjoyable."

"Well, I'm hoping to be a great mother," said Cassie, "but I have to admit I've failed at setting one of my boundaries."

Everyone stared at Cassie, the proverbial optimist who seemed to be living out her dream. "Yes, I admit it. I've failed. One of my issues is that I eat way too much sugar. The doctor is worried I might develop pre-diabetes during this pregnancy. He's warned me to be careful, and I've tried. But I'm telling you, ice cream just finds its way into my house and seriously, have you ever tasted anything as scrumptious as Abigail's brownies? I mean really. Who could stop at just one?"

Cassie passed around the Tupperware container with half the brownies gone and helped herself to another one. "That's three for me," she said. "See what I mean? Sugar is impossible to give up."

Jubilee laughed. "We'll extend you extra grace, Cassie. We understand the raging hormones of pregnancy. Once you get to the end of the final trimester, you might not even want sugar anymore."

"I doubt that," said Cassie, taking a huge bite, bits of chocolate falling in her plate.

Jubilee looked at Abigail. "And now, dear Abigail, who so gracefully wears the purple and gold scarf. What have you learned from your time in our class?"

Abigail was ready for this moment. She had thought about it ever since Jubilee had asked each of the women to bring a snack for their last meeting and be prepared to report on what the class had meant to them. How could she possibly put into one or two sentences all she had learned and how much she appreciated this incredible group of women? Her brownies as a thank you didn't seem nearly enough.

"By the way," Jubilee added, "you may take the scarf home with you tonight. I've decided to gift it to you in hopes that you will always know how beautiful you are, inside and out."

"Thank you," said Abigail as she fingered the scarf. She would hide it in a safe place until she was sure Nate would let her make more decisions about her wardrobe. Maybe under the sofa cushion. He would never look there.

She wanted desperately to tell the others about her experience with the peacock blue tank top, about how she wore that tiny sliver of material close to her heart, about how she felt defeated when she found the beautiful top in shreds. But she didn't want to monopolize the evening. This time was for celebration, not for speaking about her problems.

No, she would share one of the desires of her heart. She knew this group of women would understand.

"Thank you for all the compliments and encouragement, and thank you, Jubilee, for the gift of the scarf. It means a great deal to me. I do want you all to know how I've appreciated this class and learning to know you. I will miss our Wednesday evenings together."

Missy sniffed. Lydia handed her the Kleenex box.

Abigail smiled. "I should probably retake this class, maybe several times so I'll feel more confident. But for now, my new boundary is that I'm determined to become a teacher."

"Cool!" said Lydia.

"One of my good friends recently passed away." Abigail paused for a moment as tears for Ruth threatened to interrupt. "I miss her a great deal, because she encouraged me to seek out my dream and pursue it. She was a woman of great strength, beauty and grace and I want to be like her. I want to be courageous enough to become what God created me to be. So I guess the benefit of this class is that I'm learning how to push past my comfort zone...actually my *uncomfortable* zone, and I'm going to try with all my might to move forward in life."

"Good for you," cried Cassie. "I'm with you, friend."

The other ladies clapped and Missy crossed the room to hug Abigail. "So proud of you," she said.

Jubilee's eyes sparkled as she nodded at Abigail. "When you walk across that stage for your degree, let us know. We'll be there to cheer for you."

"Thank you," said Abigail, who felt strangely humbled and appreciated at the same time.

They spent the rest of the evening finishing the snacks, repeating some of the things Jubilee taught them and encouraging each other. At the end of the session, they held hands while Jubilee prayed an Old Testament blessing over them.

"May the Lord bless you and keep you. May the Lord make his face shine upon you and be gracious to you. May the Lord set his eyes upon you and give you peace."

※※※

When Abigail returned home, Nate was already snoring and sprawled across the bed. She stepped into the shower and sighed as the warm mist surrounded her. She squirted lavender shampoo in her hands and welcomed the calming scent. As she swirled her fingers through her hair, she practiced the self-talk she had learned during the weeks of Life Limits Class. "I am an empowered woman. How I love that word! I am a woman on a mission. I *will* discover my true self. I *will* move forward in life and someday, I *will* become a teacher."

Grateful for the noise of the shower, she added, "And I will honor Ruth by finding out what's happening at the Villas."

She turned off the water and wrapped her hair in a towel. But as she stepped onto the cold tile, she whispered, "God help me. I may have just sealed my fate."

No Visible Scars

CHAPTER TWENTY-FOUR

Abigail opened her desk drawer, found the hidden pouch and peeked at the picture of herself in the beautiful dress. Her face in the image looked excited as if she held a secret she could barely keep hidden. She stroked the paper, then carefully replaced it. Although the dress now hung safely in her closet, she liked having this hidden picture of it.

Feeling more energized, she sipped her English Breakfast tea and scrolled through emails. One was a request for additional staff at the Villa in Iowa City. Forward that one to David.

The inner office page interrupted her thoughts. Nate.

"Yes sir?"

"I'm planning another trip to Pennsylvania, this Wednesday and throughout the weekend. David is going as well, so we each need a room in the Executive Suites. We plan to ink the final deal with investors, maybe begin a new build within the next few months. Get everything ready. A reservation at the Morimoto restaurant Friday night and maybe some tickets to a baseball game on Saturday. Let me know when you're finished."

She started the process and completed it in record time, then paged Nate. "Everything is a go for your trip to

Pennsylvania." Hopefully, the Villas would soon meet the needs of residents in the Northeast.

But she cared more about unearthing why things weren't so golden in the Midwest. She needed to find the culprit and put an end to those super charges before another new site was built and residents moved in. But first, look for a confidential source who might help her.

She scrolled through the Villas website, looking at pictures of each of the staff. First up was David with his crooked grin, almost as if he was surprised the company photographer took his picture.

Nate's photo followed, light shining on his face, his red power tie perfect, that errant dark brown strand on his forehead. She flipped past it to a group picture of the Board of Directors. Samuel's white hair shone, reflecting his wisdom and powerful personality.

She ignored her own picture, then clicked back to it. The hair she hated so much hung down both sides of her face, and her smile seemed plastic. Her white blouse and black blazer added nothing except a feeling of depression. She gazed at her eyes on the screen and wondered if anyone else saw the hidden pain. Maybe it was because she knew herself better now and understood what lay behind the scenes.

Behind the scenes. That was it.

The one employee who thrived on working behind the scenes. In fact, that's what he called himself, "Behind the Scenes Ralph." The auditor who showed up once a year to make sure everything was ready for tax season. Quiet, yet self-assured. Trust-worthy. The exact source to help her unlock this mystery.

She sent him a quick email. "Ralph, I need to examine a few details regarding a request from a friend of mine. Could you come to the office this Thursday morning?"

The reply came quickly, "Sure. I'll be there at nine sharp."

Thursday. With Nate and David safely in Pennsylvania, Abigail would be in charge of the front office. This was the perfect time to dig into the official records and find out what was going on.

❧❧❧

Thursday morning, Abigail called Cassie before she left for work. Cassie sounded as if she had just crawled out of bed. "Yeah? Hmm. Do you know how early it is?"

"Barely six thirty, and I'm on my way to the office. I need to stop by your house and get my wig."

"Your what?"

"My wig. You know, the auburn bob you're hiding for me. Just hand it to me at your front door, and I won't bother you with anything else."

"Okay. But...why?"

"I'll explain later."

Abigail finished getting ready for work, then drove to Cassie's. She circled around the massive drive, smiled at the pile of mulch that stood in a corner of the front yard. Rick was always busy landscaping for everybody else and finished prepping his own yard last.

No Visible Scars

At the front door, Cassie's hand reached out with a plastic sack. "I'm a real mess. Didn't sleep well."

"Sorry." Abigail opened the door wider and noted Cassie's puffy eyes, her robe buttoned crooked. "Thanks, friend." She kissed Cassie's cheek. "Later."

"You'd better believe it. I love a mystery. Coffee tomorrow at the Happy Grounds?"

"Yep. See ya'."

At the office, Abigail scurried to the ladies room and fished her wig out of the sack. Once in place, she surveyed her reflection and suddenly felt a burst of empowerment. She would deal with Ralph in a businesslike fashion, as if the newly-emerging Abigail had finally crawled out of her cocoon.

Exactly at nine o'clock, Ralph walked through the front office door. He nodded and said, "Shall we meet in the conference room?"

"Certainly. I've already turned on the Keurig."

She followed Ralph, noticing the way he bounced along with a clipped gait. His bald spot made a perfect oval in the back of his head, yet his stance and his walk seemed like a much younger man. The ultimate professional who understood the company's finances on every level. A trusted confidante. Hopefully.

Ralph laid his briefcase on the table, clicked it open and pulled out his Macbook Air. Then he chose a K-cup from the selection on the counter and inserted it into the Keurig. The gurgling of hot water echoed through the conference room.

"Something hot for you?" asked Ralph.

"No, thank you." Her stomach felt like a churning load of angry laundry, roiling around through the cleansing cycle. She reached up to fluff her bangs and thought of the empowerment she felt earlier. The image of Jubilee and the other ladies in class surrounding her in the giant mirror. She could do this. With Ralph's help, maybe they would solve this puzzle and fulfill Ruth's last request.

She cleared her throat and began. "I need to ask you to keep what I'm going to tell you completely confidential. This is just between the two of us, until we find out exactly what's going on. Can I count on your discretion?"

He reached into his shirt pocket for his reading glasses, unfolded them and placed them on his nose. "Of course. Why don't you tell me what this is about?"

She began with Ruth's concern for her friend, then recited what the directors at the various Villas had told her. "I don't know everything about the company's finances, and I don't need to know it all. I just want to find out if something unethical or illegal is going on— something we can fix so the residents will be able to enjoy their activities without extra charges. And...." She swallowed hard. "Ruth was my friend. I want to honor her by fulfilling her final request."

Ralph pecked away on his keyboard, occasionally looking up as he listened to her concerns. When she finished, he stared at her so long, she wondered if her wig had slipped. Then he pushed a few more keys and said, "Hmm. This may be it. But nothing really damaging. No real proof."

He pushed the laptop toward her but all she could see were figures, charts, pluses and minuses, a few red numbers, but mostly black. "I don't get it."

Ralph stood. He picked up a company pen lying on the table and pointed at several figures on the laptop's screen. "See here? There's a small charge for a Bible study activity at the Villa in Illinois. Another charge for a painting class in Overland Park."

"Yes." Her heart pumped faster. "That's probably the one for Ruth's friend."

"Hmm. Apparently, these small charges appear throughout the fiscal year, but only in bits. Nothing really adds up, especially if you're not looking for it. And, of course, we wouldn't pay attention to fifteen dollars per month at one facility for a seemingly inconsequential activity. However...." He poked at more keys. Various charts danced across the screen.

"Hmm." Then as another chart appeared, "Oh my." Then "Crap!" and finally "Damn it all!" His face turned red as he plopped into one of the leather chairs. "There's a discrepancy in the books. I'm sure I would have discovered it at some point before our next audit. But I wouldn't have known how to attribute it without your knowledge. I am appalled, but thank you."

"I don't quite understand. Forgive my ignorance. You're saying there's a discrepancy, but how much? Is it a major amount? And is there any way of proving where it's coming from?"

He took a deep breath, seemed to suck as much oxygen as possible from the room. "On a monthly scale from one location to another, it isn't a major catastrophe. But when you multiply the small amounts by the number of Villas we own and then factor in the annual report for the entire fiscal year...it comes to...." Ralph punched a few more keys. "Twelve thousand, five hundred and four dollars and...eighteen cents."

"Wow!"

"Indeed. Again, not a major financial disaster by any means when we're talking about all the assets of the Villas de Comfort. But twelve thousand adds up over time and taken in little pieces, who knows how long this has been going on? I could probably do a historical search over the last five years and see what we're dealing with. Would you like me to do that?"

"Yes, please." She felt sick and hoped she wouldn't have to run to the ladies room. She looked at Ralph's screen again. "But can you tell where these numbers began? I mean, is there a way to find out who is doing this?"

He nodded. "Everything is coded and only the top executives know how the codes work. When I pull the numbers for the annual audit, I pull them by codes. That's how I might have missed this. If I didn't access the code, then those additional charges might have stayed hidden for perpetuity. You have done us a great service, ma'am, by bringing this to our attention."

She noticed the use of the plural pronoun and again hoped Ralph would not divulge her clandestine search to Nate. But she wanted another question answered. "You mentioned only the top executives know the codes. Exactly who would that be?"

Ralph stared at her for a moment. "Myself, of course. Then also the CEO...."

David. No surprise there.

"...and the President of the Board of Directors."

Samuel. It seemed ludicrous that Samuel might be involved.

Ralph cleared his throat. "And one more." He stared at Abigail. "The other executive who knows the codes would be your husband, Mr. Calebian."

Although she knew it was a possibility Nate might have mismanaged the books, the reality made her sick. And the worst part was that she knew at some point, if she kept her promise to Ruth, she would have to confront him.

Her mouth felt dry. She stood up and walked to the office fridge, pulled out a bottle of Pellegrino and drank several gulps. Then she squared her shoulders and walked slowly back toward Ralph. "Can you show me these codes? I don't need to know all of them, but can you show me the code used for these excess charges?"

"I can show some of it to you, but it's rather a puzzle. It doesn't line up with the rest of the spectrum. Another reason why it was easy to hide these amounts."

He punched more keys, then brought up a window with several alphabet letters and numbers. "You'll notice the first two letters are abbreviations for the states as in IL for Illinois, IA for Iowa, KS for Kansas, et cetera. Then we have a dash and the initials of the person who authorized the charges. This setup protects us so we can always go back and find out who to ask if there's a discrepancy. Here's a charge authorized by your husband, NC, for the Villa in Missouri.

So we have MO-NC at the beginning, then a series of numbers which includes the date of the authorization and the zip code of the location. Therefore, MO-NC-110912-63015."

"Clever."

"Thank you. I devised this system my first week on the job. It has served us well. However, we now have this strange code that has been inserted." He sighed and opened another screen which Abigail recognized as an electronic bank register.

"Hmm...although these charges have been coded in and registered on our accounts, there is no record they have been stolen from our bank account. In other words, we're not really talking about fraud. Whoever is doing this, is actually making extra money for the company, not taking money for himself."

Abigail exhaled and the knot in her stomach seemed to ease. She rolled her shoulders, trying to ease the tension. "So...it's nothing illegal, but it *is* unethical, right? It's overcharging in order to make more of a profit. Correct?"

"Yes, ma'am. That's it."

At least she wouldn't have to call the police and report one of her superiors, possibly her husband. But it still made her sad that the residents and their families were being overcharged, and some of the residents could no longer participate in their favorite activities. Samuel and the Board of Directors would be highly displeased.

"Thank you, Ralph, but we still don't know who is behind this, do we?"

"Not until we break this strange code." He pulled up the previous window and pointed toward the extra charge at the facility in Illinois. "It begins innocently enough, but then after the dash, we have this series of letters which refer to no one on the executive team. See it here? IL for Illinois, but then LSPB. What does that mean? Then the date makes sense. 090515, but instead of a zip code, 0826. What that means, I have no idea."

She felt gut punched and rubbed her stomach. She took several moments to breathe deep breaths, then found her voice. "I'm not sure about the LSPB but the 0826 is the last four digits of my husband's social security number."

So Nate was definitely fiddling with the accounts. His 0826 was as clear as a thumb print. Abigail forced herself to numb down her emotions. She needed to think. LSPB. What sort of code would Nate put together, using those letters?

"Wait a minute," she said. "My husband has a practice he uses with all his passwords and he taught me to do it as well. He reverses the letters of his last name to make it harder for hackers to get into his account. So if he used the same tactic here, then LSPB reversed would become BPSL."

"But what is the meaning of those letters?" Ralph punched keys and pulled up more charts.

Abigail paced to the end of the room, then back. She straightened a pile of letterhead paper on the table. The tagline of the Villas de Comfort across the top of the page: The Best Place for Senior Living.

She exhaled and picked up a page of letterhead, thrust it toward Ralph. "Here it is. The initials that represent our tagline. BPSL. He reversed those letters and included the last four of his social. It couldn't be more clear if he had signed his name."

Ralph's blue eyes seemed to soften. "That makes sense. I'm sorry. This must be a blow...to realize your husband...."

"Yes, well...." She thought about Ruth who once told her, "The fruit identifies the tree." But Ruth was talking about her husband and what a good man he was. Good fruit didn't apply to Nate.

"Thank you again, Ralph, for all your help. I'll think about this and decide what our next steps need to be. Let's keep everything about this meeting a secret between us."

Ralph packed up his Mac, clicked his briefcase shut and strode toward the conference room door. Then he turned back. "You can depend on my discretion."

Abigail sat in the conference room for several moments. She breathed deep breaths and tried to calm herself. The mystery was solved, but now she would have to tell David and eventually, confront Nate.

She pressed her hands to the wig and remembered the feeling of empowerment when she slipped it on. A vision of Ruth in her colorful afghans. Ruth, mentor and friend, sharing her tea and her wisdom.

Abigail stood, her shoulders pulled back with pride and self-confidence. She would do what she had to do—for Ruth and for herself.

No Visible Scars

CHAPTER TWENTY-FIVE

The weekend passed quickly. Nate returned with glowing reports about the visits with investors in Pennsylvania. "We inked the contract and next month, we'll look for bids on construction for the new site. Sam and the board ought to be pleased with my handling of this new contract."

"And David?" Abigail asked. "Was he pleased as well?"

"Sure. He found a music store that had some sort of mandolin he's been looking for. All he cares about are those stupid poems he writes and how he makes them into songs. Biggest waste of time."

She stirred a pan of chicken with white beans and green chilies. She added chopped cilantro, then put the lid on the pan and turned toward the cabinets to pull out the dinner dishes.

"Mmm," said Nate, his arm encircling her waist. "Smells good."

Abigail shivered. She stepped away and pulled open the fridge door. "Cheese. Where's the cheese?"

"Get back here," he said. He grabbed her wrist and twisted it. Then his mouth clamped over hers, claiming her, demanding from her what she knew she had to give, especially if she wanted to find out what was going on at the Villas. No sense making him suspicious.

She had read on the internet how making love in the kitchen was a great way to kindle romance. But after Nate finished, she thought about writing her own article about the difference between sex and love. In her opinion, nothing about a hard kitchen floor represented romance.

They ate dinner quietly with an occasional grunt of satisfaction from Nate. "Lots better than those dumb old brownies you're always making. Cook this stuff more often." He patted his stomach and yawned. "Think I'll take a little nap. I'm beat."

He stretched out on his recliner while she finished cleaning up the dishes. She squirted Mister Clean on the floor, bent down on her hands and knees and rubbed the antiseptic every place Nate might have touched.

Tears streamed down her face as she wished she could rub all the bad memories from her mind. The way he grabbed her wrist. A small purple spot already showed and would probably take several days to fade. The way he forced himself on her, not stopping even when she cried out from the pain of his forceful advances. She felt humiliated, violated, as if he prostituted her. Maybe she should have asked him to leave a tip.

After she finished cleaning, she checked to make sure Nate was snoring in his recliner. She crept downstairs to the office, moved the vacuum cleaner that stood in the doorway and powered up the computer. Nate kept a file in his Excel account, all his user names and passwords with his system of reversing letters. She printed out one of the pages in the file to use as hard proof when she spoke with David.

She heard a sound, then "Abby? Where are you?" His steps on the stairs. Hide the paper. But where?

She shut down the computer and folded the paper, then remembered the vacuum cleaner. She lifted the top of the canister and slipped the paper inside, clicking it shut just as he appeared at the office door.

"What are you doing down here? It's time for bed."

"Just straightening up." She held up the hose end of the vacuum. "The maid obviously left this out and I knew you would want a clean office. Just trying to think of you, dear." Another lie. She was beyond caring.

He looked toward the computer. The black screen stared back. "Well, hurry up. I'm going to bed, and I want you lying next to me."

"Be up in a minute." She rose on her tiptoes to peck his cheek.

He grinned, then turned and climbed the stairs.

She stood for a minute, still holding the vacuum hose. Was this the best place to hide an incriminating paper? Nate always vacuumed his own car. But he rarely changed the dirty bag inside for a new one. Surely the paper would be safe for a few hours.

She wound the hose around the vacuum and placed it in the closet. She would wait until he left for the office in the morning, then retrieve the hidden paper.

Upstairs, she took off her makeup and brushed through her hair. Nate wrestled around and thumped his

No Visible Scars

pillows. Hopefully, he would fall asleep soon and she could rest peacefully.

One of his business cards lay on the bedside table. She picked it up and felt the nubby engraving. Her husband's name next to Villas de Comfort with the scrolling tagline underneath: The Best Place for Senior Living. Not such a great place in the Corporate office.

⁂

The next morning, she fixed Nate's breakfast, then sat across from him as she munched on her toast and a banana. "I'll be at work a bit later," she said. "I need to finish putting supper in the crock pot. It will only take a half hour or so."

He frowned. "Why didn't you get up earlier to do that? You've got to plan ahead. Think, for once."

"You're right, of course. Next time."

He finished eating, then grabbed his briefcase and hurried out the door. She waited until his car turned the curve out of their subdivision. Then she quickly threw some vegetables into the crock pot, poured in some chicken stock and flicked the crock pot setting to "Slow."

She hurried downstairs to the office, reached into the vacuum for the incriminating paper. Was she doing the right thing? She shook her head. Stop second guessing herself. Jubilee might not like the secretive methods, but Ruth would chuckle about them. Cassie would be proud of her. But she wanted to be proud of herself. She was getting tired of all the deception.

Upstairs, she rolled the paper into a tube shape and tucked it inside a tampon. Nate might check her purse, but he would never mess with her feminine hygiene products.

When she walked into the office, a strumming sound greeted her. David's new mandolin. She sat quietly for a moment and listened to the mellow sound. If only she could sit in his office for a while and revel in his latest composition. But she had work to do.

First, make sure Nate was occupied. She clicked the inner office button. "Just checking in. Anything I can get for you this morning?"

"Coffee. Black. Dave and I have a meeting soon. In my office."

She fixed two coffees, in case David wanted one, and carried them to Nate's office. Then she returned to her desk and waited until she heard both their voices engaged in conversation. She reached for her purse, carefully unrolled the hidden paper and placed it inside a manila folder labeled Miscellaneous. Then she filed the folder behind the Michigan personnel files.

Why did Nate feel the need to steal from residents and feed into a company that operated so far in the black? They were already headed for the Forbes 500 of successful businesses. Maybe it was the same need that filtered everything around his egotistical desires. She hated to admit how much he had deceived the company, David, the shareholders, Samuel and the board. Yet, she had continued with this search because of her promise to Ruth. She needed only to face the final resolution.

She checked Nate's schedule for the next visit to an out-of-state site. Illinois, next Monday afternoon through Wednesday morning. She had one week to gather all the incriminating paperwork, then present the evidence to David. Make it as simple as possible, then let David take it from there.

She reserved the flights and Nate's itinerary, set up everything as she knew he would want. He would depart 12:01, just after noon on Monday, probably order a special lunch delivered to the office before he left. He hated airline food. Then he would return Wednesday evening at 5:37, in time to expect a meal on the table when he arrived home. Unless he expected her to pick him up at the airport. In that case, he would want to eat out, to celebrate whatever wonderful things he had accomplished at the Villa in Illinois.

She considered her window of time. She needed to carefully plan everything so all the pieces fell into place. Then leave it up to fate or God to work it all out. God...where was he in all of this? Maybe he helped her find Jubilee and the Life Limits Class. Maybe Cassie and those women represented the catalyst she needed to wake up, to help her realize she didn't have to live within a dangerous marriage. Did God want her to stay with this man, to continue with this life? If she left, would God judge her?

She shook her head, then combed through her hair with her fingers. No need to think about God right now or try to figure out theological arguments. She had work to do.

First, email Ralph. "Please print off all documents related to LSPB0826 and fax to me next Monday afternoon at 2:30 p.m. No sooner, please."

A response from Ralph returned within seconds. "Copy that. Will do."

She quickly deleted all emails to Ralph.

Check David's schedule for next Tuesday. In the office all day. Schedule a time to meet with him and present all the evidence.

Next, text Cassie. After her meeting with Ralph, she had hidden the wig again at Cassie's house. To feel completely empowered and confident, she would need it when she met with David. "Tuesday...need wig again. Will pick it up Monday night. This time, I'll keep it."

Cassie texted back with a happy face.

Figure out a way to deal with the fallout from Nate. If there were any repercussions from her discussions with Ralph and David, Nate would take it out on her.

Cassie had offered a place to stay if the relationship worsened. Hopefully, nothing drastic would happen. For now, she just had to survive this week, get all her ducks in a row and prepare to tell David the truth.

In spite of her worries, she stayed focused at the office and counted off the days until Nate left. Every night, she ticked through the list of things she would tell David and what she needed to prepare. "I can do this," she whispered.

On Monday, she and Nate shared an early lunch at Quizno's, then she dropped him at the airport and accepted his peck on her cheek. "Make sure you stay close to the phone and the computer," he said, "just in case I need anything while I'm out of the office."

"Sure. I know the drill." As she drove onto the I-35 ramp, she accelerated with a strange sense of loss. The next time she saw him, her part in this nightmare would be over. David would possess the evidence.

She took the traffic-swollen ramp toward Metcalf. The first score of the "Mission Impossible" theme pounded through her brain. She wished she could shut it off or at least turn down the volume. She never imagined herself living in a thriller movie, and she doubted if the final scene would end happily ever after.

※※※

Ralph was as punctual as Abigail expected. At exactly two thirty, his fax came through with eleven pages worth of line items for LSPB0826. She filed them in the Miscellaneous folder, then scheduled a meeting with David for Tuesday morning at nine, disguised as "Possible Investor" on the Outlook calendar.

David responded with a green tag: Confirmed.

At the end of her work day, she drove to Cassie's house to pick up the wig. "Come on in," said Cassie. "I'm just putting the finishing touches on supper. You want to join us?" Cassie waddled from cabinet to sink, her pregnant belly arriving ahead of her.

"No, thanks. I'm so nervous, I don't think I could eat."

"So tomorrow's the big day you're going to present everything to David?"

"Yes. Everything is ready. Except me. I'll work on that in the morning. I have to look and feel my best. I'm making some brownies, because I know David loves them. I just hope he'll accept what I have to say without getting mad."

Cassie looked puzzled. "Has David ever been mad at you?"

"No, but we're talking about the company he co-founded. And if, by some mistake, I'm confused about this or wrongly accusing Nate, everything could go terribly wrong. I could lose my marriage, my home, my livelihood—everything."

"I doubt that's going to happen. They need you in that front office and as for your marriage…well…."

"I know. It's not much of a marriage, is it?" She suddenly felt bereft of all the hopes and dreams she once held as a young bride.

Cassie hugged her and the baby kicked. Both of them squealed. "That's a good sign," said Cassie. "See? The baby is excited and encouraging you to forge ahead. Do what's right. Tell David the truth, then no matter what happens, begin living your own life."

"I guess you're right. I just need extra courage to carry it out."

"You know what Jubilee would say."

"What?"

Cassie's eyes twinkled. "We're all afraid at some point, but we find our strength when we forge ahead. Do it afraid."

She placed her hand on Cassie's protruding belly. "Thank you, little one." Then she hugged Cassie. "And thank you, friend."

No Visible Scars

CHAPTER TWENTY-SIX

Abigail laid the beautiful dress on her bed. The ruche waist, the brilliant blue swirls, the silky fabric. She set out her black Gucci heels, then pulled the wig out of the sack and set it on the bedpost.

Might as well go downstairs and make the brownies. She planned to bake a double batch and assembled all the ingredients. The chocolate chips were in the freezer because they always cooked better if they started out cold. She helped herself to a handful. Nothing quite as wonderful as frozen chocolate.

With the brownies in the oven, she poured herself a glass of Merlot and sat on the love seat in the sunroom. A picture of Nate stood on top of the étagère in the corner. Sadness spread over her. Once Nate found out what she had done, she would have to move out and create a new identity. But at least she would leave with a clear conscience, knowing she had kept her promise to Ruth. She would find a new job somewhere, maybe on campus, close to her dream. As Jubilee would say, forge ahead.

She finished her wine, then left the glass on the floor knowing it would irk Nate when he found it. She didn't care about his stupid rules anymore. It was all or nothing.

The oven dinged. She stuck a toothpick in the brownies. Perfect. In the morning, she would carefully place them on a plate and seal them with plastic wrap. Moist and rich, exactly as David liked them.

She checked all the security codes for the house, then slowly climbed the stairs to get ready for bed.

Please God. Help me sleep.

No way could she impress David, even in her new dress, if she wore dark circles under her eyes.

※※※

She woke before the alarm, grateful she had slept for several hours. She felt energized and ready for whatever the day held. After her shower, she carefully applied her makeup and pinned her hair on top of her head. Then she pulled the wig on and stood a minute admiring herself in the mirror. The auburn strands with a few chestnut highlights so perfect for her skin tone. George was right. If she lived through this, she would make an appointment with the salon. Strip out the nasty blonde and go back to her natural color.

As she slipped the dress over her head, inner strength began to seep into every pore. She chanted to herself, remembering the ladies from Life Limits Class and the confidence they shared with her, "Ab-i-gail, Ab-i-gail. Source of joy. Freedom and strength—that's me."

She adjusted the bodice and stood in front of the mirror wishing she could have a dress like this in every color. Every color, that is, except black, white or beige. "I can do this," she told her image. "I'm doing this for Ruth, and for every resident who has been cheated by my husband."

As she thought of Nate and the fear of what he might do to her, bile settled in her throat. She coughed, then reminded herself, "I can do this." She put the emphasis on each word. "*I* can do this. I *can* do this. I can *do* this. I can do *this*. God, help me."

In her black Gucci heels, the auburn wig and the flowing dress, she descended the spiral staircase and stood elegantly at the bottom rung. "I *will* do this. For Ruth. And… for myself."

She hurried into the kitchen and brewed some Earl Grey tea, sipped a bit to steady her nerves and prayed for the caffeine to kick in. She popped a couple of red grapes in her mouth, then settled on a slice of cheese. Protein to feed the brain. She carefully placed the brownies in the center of her favorite Pottery Barn platter and surrounded them with clusters of the red grapes. A few pieces of Ghirardelli dark chocolate filled in the gaps. She finished with plastic wrap around the platter, grabbed her purse and headed for the garage.

When she reached the office, she quickly retrieved the Miscellaneous folder and studied the papers she would show David. She booted up her computer and checked her Inbox, noting several emails from Nate. It seemed ironic to send replies to him, to act as if everything was normal when she was about to reveal his corruption. Her hands shook as she moved the mouse across the page.

At eight forty-five, David still had not arrived. She checked a few emails, then watched the digital clock in the corner of her computer screen change to eight forty-eight, forty-nine, fifty. At eight fifty-two, she heard the ding of the elevator. A few moments later, David opened the door and hurried inside the office.

As he passed her desk, he stared at his phone. Abigail felt slightly relieved. He hadn't noticed the wig nor the striking color of her dress. She would own the element of surprise when she walked into his office. That would give her the advantage.

The clock changed to nine o'clock and David buzzed the office intercom. "Is our guest here, Abigail? Show him or her in, please."

She picked up the platter of food and the recriminating folder of information, then tried to quiet the thumping of her heart. She walked down the hallway to David's office.

"I can do this," she whispered as she rapped on the door.

"Come in, please."

She turned the doorknob and stepped into David's office. He stood behind his desk, then came forward with his hand extended. "How do you do?" Then he stopped and gaped. "Abigail? Is that you?"

"Yes, and I've brought you some treats."

He took the plate, but didn't even look at the brownies or the carefully arranged grapes and chocolate. He continued to stare as she met his gaze. The thumping of her heart lessened as she felt adrenaline surge through her veins. She squared her shoulders and asked, "Would you like me to get you some coffee?"

"Uh...no. Is the investor coming?"

"I'm afraid I've misled you a bit, because I wanted to be certain you would be in the office today. No investor is scheduled for this time slot. Only me. I have something very important to show you."

"Uh...okay." He placed the platter on his desk, then motioned toward the chairs across from his desk. "Shall we sit?"

For a second, she thought about it. Then she decided to use a ploy she read in a WE magazine. Always stand when you need to exhibit a sign of power. "You may sit if you'd like, but I'll stand."

"Okay." David seemed lost for words. He looked down at the platter. "Brownies. Thanks. I'll...uh...eat them later."

She flipped open the folder. "You may remember I often visited your great grandmother, Ruth. She was a wonderful woman, a mentor to me."

"Yes. She told me. I miss her." His eyes filled, and he cleared his throat.

"So do I. But before she died, I promised her I would look into something that troubled her. That's what I want to share with you this morning."

He looked puzzled. "Granny Ruth was troubled about something? Why didn't she tell me?"

"I don't know. Perhaps it just slipped out over our tea time, or maybe she didn't want to worry you with it. She was always thinking of others." Abigail felt her throat tighten and willed herself not to cry, not even in remembrance of Ruth.

"Go on," David said with a puzzled look on his face.

"Ruth told me some of her friends were being charged for activities at the Villas. Some of the craft activities and Bible studies were being charged to their accounts, and they were concerned about it."

"We've never charged extra for those things."

Abigail nodded. "At first I thought Ruth's friend might be confused. I researched the problem, talked to other directors. I asked Ralph to help me because I didn't want to bother you about it until I knew exactly what we were dealing with. Nate isn't aware that I'm talking to you about this or that Ralph has checked the figures and found damaging evidence."

David walked behind his desk, pulled out his leather chair and sat down. He ran his fingers through his hair and took a deep breath. "Go on."

She moved closer and pushed several papers toward him. "Ralph noticed one of the codes was a bit different than the others." She pointed to a line on the print-out. "This line represents the code that's out of place."

"It's completely different from our usual code. What does it mean?"

"It took me a while, but knowing Nate and his system of backwards passwords...."

"Yeah, he did that in college."

"I'm not surprised." She handed him another paper. "If you'll look at his home files, he does the same thing. The backwards passwords and codes, almost like a signature."

"Okay. So Nate has this system with password codes. What does that have to do with the Villas and over-charging residents?" He reached for a brownie and took a bite. "Mmm. I didn't have breakfast this morning. Thanks."

"You're welcome." She fished another paper from the pile. "Ralph has totaled up these budget lines for LSPB0826. As one or two lines, it doesn't seem like much. But over time, it adds up to thousands of dollars."

"Thousands? What is LSPB0826?"

She handed him a copy of the company letterhead. "It's an acrostic for our tagline, 'The Best Place for Senior Living'. BPSL in reverse."

"Clever. And the 0826?"

"The last four digits of Nate's social security number."

David stood up and stared out the window of his corner office. Then he slowly turned, his fists clenched. "Nate went behind my back and ordered charges for these activities, then coded them so he would know how much was coming in?"

"Exactly. He didn't steal any of the money for himself. It isn't exactly fraud, but...."

"But it isn't right. It takes advantage of our residents and their families. Why would Nate do this?"

"I'm not sure, except he's always been proud of the money he earns and what he brings to the company. Maybe he thought this would be a boost for the company or a stroke for his pride. I hate to think at some point he was going to steal the money and hide it in a separate account."

David's face began to turn red, then he pounded his fist on the desk. One of the grapes bounced to the floor. Abigail stooped to pick it up.

He started to pace. "We've been headed for a battle. He was so mad when I was appointed CEO, but this...this thievery and this sneaking around behind my back...this fiddling with the books. And after everything we've been through together...all the ways we've worked together for so long...I won't stand for it. I'll fire him. No, I'll kill him."

Abigail shook her head. "You can't do that. You're the CEO now, and as angry as you are, you've got to think about the company and the role you play. Everything depends on you keeping a level head. It's true that Nate did something foolish, but it won't help matters if you call him out and clobber him. Think about the bad press for the company."

He walked to the window, looked out on the morning skyline. "You're right, but something needs to be done. He has to pay for this. I'll fire him. I have the authority to do that."

"Yes, but is that a wise decision? Nate is one of the best business developers in the state, maybe one of the top ten in the country. He knows how to sell the concept of the Villas to investors. In fact, he's the one who made sure the Pennsylvania deal went through. If you fire him, who will take his place?"

David stormed over to his desk and twirled the Rolodex. He stopped at a certain card, then lifted the office phone and punched in a number. After a few seconds, he said, "Ralph. I need you at the office. Now."

Several more pacings back and forth, then he stopped and moved closer to Abigail. He reached out and put his hand on her shoulder. "Thank you. This couldn't have been easy for you to tell me. What you've said has a lot of wisdom in it, and I'll think about it. When is Nate scheduled to come back in the office?"

"He flies home tomorrow night. He'll be here on Thursday."

"That gives me plenty of time to talk to Ralph and put together a plan. We can't allow this to go on. But you're right. I have to be careful about the reputation of the company and Nate *is* a valuable employee. Well-known in the community. I'll figure out something that will make this situation beneficial to the Villas yet send a strong statement about our ethics. We'll start by refunding every penny to the residents."

Abigail nodded. "I think that's a good first step. Ruth would be proud of you."

He took her hand and squeezed it. "Thank you again. I'll keep you posted. And thanks for the brownies and...everything."

She turned to go. She felt as if a great weight had suddenly lifted off her shoulders.

Before she reached the door, David said, "Abigail."

"Yes?" She turned around.

His crooked grin lit his face. "Love the dress...and the hair."

"Thank you. So do I."

Back at her desk, she breathed deeply then reached for the secret pouch and the picture hidden within. She pulled it out and tossed it in the trash. No need to hide anymore. She had completed her mission, told David what he needed to know and worn her new look with dignity. She was ready to be her authentic self.

※ ※ ※

As David waited for Ralph, he sat with his head in his hands. The anger slowly drained and in its place, self-recrimination poured in. How could he not have seen this? Of all the people in the Villas Corporate, he should have known what his college buddy was capable of. Maybe he wasn't worthy of being CEO after all.

A brief knock on the door. He squared his shoulders. "Come in."

Ralph entered, briefcase in hand and walked straight toward the seating area. "I assume you have spoken to Mrs. Calebian. You know about the situation?"

"Yes. You and I will be working throughout the day and maybe late tonight. We'll look at all the finances and find any places where Nate might have siphoned funds from the residents. Are you ready?"

Ralph powered up his Mac. "Of course. He used a clever system, but since Mrs. Calebian figured out the code, it's been easy to track."

"Thank God she stepped in and let us know. I want this entire thing rooted out and dealt with immediately."

"Of course."

Another rap on the door. Abigail entered, two mugs and a coffee carafe in her hands. "I assumed you might need a caffeine fix."

"Thank you," David said, "and hold all my calls today. This matter is top priority. I know we can depend on you."

As she exited the office, Ralph stared at the closed door. "A beautiful woman," he said.

"Yes. And smart. We're fortunate to have her. Now, let's get to work."

※※※

Ralph left at eleven thirty that night, but David stayed in the office. He finished off the brownies, then started on the grapes with another cup of coffee. Abigail. What a woman! She had put herself in danger. He knew that. He hadn't been blind all these years. He saw how she often seemed afraid of Nate. He just hadn't known what to do about it.

He and Ralph had worked out a plan and in the next couple of days, David would share that plan with Samuel. But first, he would confront Nate as soon as he came into the office on Thursday morning. He would show him the paperwork Abigail provided and more numbers Ralph had printed out. The evidence was damning. If Nate hadn't been so persistent about using backward codes, he might never have been caught.

But David would show him the proof and dare Nate to prove him wrong. He owed him that much.

Abigail was right. Nate was good at his job, but developers could be taught. Maybe it was time to introduce some new blood into the Villas. Change things up a bit. With a new corporate structure, the Villas could go even farther in the years to come. He longed to see that scenario played out.

He would insist that Nate begin training a younger version of himself, some kid with an MBA who respected older folks. They had plenty of resumes in the office files from college grads who wanted a chance to prove their worth. Training his own replacement would be one of the consequences for Nate.

Ralph would sit in on those training sessions and make sure everything was on the up and up. Then eventually, when the new kid learned the ropes, David would quietly ask for Nate's resignation. In spite of their past together, he no longer trusted his old friend.

But what would happen to Abigail? He didn't want her to leave. She was an outstanding executive assistant and in that amazing dress.... He tried to ignore the images that flashed through his mind.

She was, after all, Nate's wife, and she was strong enough to stand up to him. She certainly showed courage coming into his office and telling him the truth. He had to give her plenty of bonus points for that.

What would Nate do if he found out his wife had turned him in? David certainly wouldn't tell him and neither would Ralph. He was sure of that. He clenched his jaw. If Nate ever hurt that woman, David would wring his neck. He didn't care if he *was* the CEO with responsibilities to the company. He wouldn't put up with that kind of abuse, not from one of his employees.

The first rays of morning sunshine peeked over the horizon. Tomorrow at this time, he would confront Nate. How everything played out from that point, only God knew. David looked at the changing colors in the sky and thought of Granny Ruth. How he missed her! He knew she would be proud of him for sticking to his principles and making sure everything was done right.

He walked across his office and picked up the mandolin leaning against his bookcase. As he strummed the strings and adjusted the frets, he hummed the tune he had worked on for several weeks. Thank God for the soothing joy of music. This morning, with Nate on his mind and the image of Abigail in her flowing dress still fresh, he needed some relief. No one was in the office this early. He could sing as loud as he wanted.

"You, oh God, are my refuge and my strength.
You are present even in this time of trouble.
So I will not be afraid. I will stand strong.
Even if the world disappears and everything changes
You, oh God, are the same.
I will be still and listen for you
Because you are my God and the One I trust."

As the echoes of the song reverberated around his office, David felt renewed and refreshed. No matter what happened from this point forward, he would trust God to help him with all the details. Even if he had to replace Nate and say good-bye to Abigail, he would do it for the sake of the company and for the memory of Granny Ruth.

It was time to truly embrace his role as CEO, to use his power to make a difference in the world of assisted living. He was determined to do it with his heart in the right place and his mind clear.

He picked up his cell phone and punched the number for the florist. He hadn't ordered any flowers since Granny Ruth died and he wasn't sure exactly what Abigail liked. He knew she liked blue, now that he had seen that dress, but he couldn't think of any blue flowers. She had just saved the company, so he had to thank her. Only heaven knew how much it had cost her.

A sleepy voice answered. "May I help you?"

"Yes. I'd like to order a dozen roses…red, I guess…to be delivered this morning to Abigail Calebian at the Villas de Comfort corporate office. Sign the card "With gratitude for your excellent work.""

"Yes, sir. Right away."

"You have my credit card in the system. This is David Judah, CEO."

CHAPTER TWENTY-SEVEN

On Wednesday morning, Abigail shuffled papers at her desk, dressed in her usual taupe blouse, black slacks and blazer. When she picked up Nate at the airport, he would know she came straight from the office. No need to invite his anger about her clothes. Better to appear professional. Business as usual.

But carefully pinned to her bra was the colorful peacock blue strip of fabric. She could feel it when she touched her chest. It would give her the strength she needed for this day.

She fixed a cup of hot tea and straightened everything on her desk. David strummed a song in his office. It was wonderful how he chose that type of artistic release. If only she could find something like that for herself.

Her days as executive assistant were probably numbered. She patted herself on the shoulder. She could move forward in life, be her true self and find a way to live authentically. Life Limits Class and Ruth had taught her to respect herself.

Around 11:30, a delivery came. A bouquet of red roses with white baby's breath scattered among the crimson petals. The delivery boy, who looked to be a high school kid, read the name on the card. "Abigail Calebian. Is that you?"

"Why...yes."

The kid grinned and set the crystal vase on her desk. "Have a wonderful day." Then he hurried out the door.

"Thank you." She read the card and smelled the aroma of the roses, drinking in their scent. She giggled, then straightened her blazer, checked her hair in the reflection of the Monet painting and walked toward David's office.

His door was open. He stood behind his desk with the mandolin in his hand.

"I don't know how to thank you," she said. "The roses are lovely."

"I'm the one thanking you. You've earned an entire bush of roses...and more." A slight frown between his eyes. "No blue dress today? And your hair? It must have been a wig."

She nodded. "I'm dressed for my husband today. The way he likes me to look."

"Hmm." He looked as if he didn't know what to say. Abigail felt a bit speechless herself. He cleared his throat. "I want you to know what I'm planning to do."

Her heart began to drum.

"As soon as Nate gets into the office tomorrow morning, I'll meet with him. I've asked Ralph to come in as well and together, we'll confront him with all the evidence. Give him a chance to explain. I'm not going to mention your name in any of this. Whether or not you tell him, that's up to you. And, as you requested, I'll keep Nate on as our COO and Chief Development Officer until we can train someone else."

"That sounds fair." A validation. David agreed with her and appreciated her opinion. Relief rushed through her, and she sighed inwardly.

"But Abigail...are you going to be all right? Is there anything else I can do for you?"

"Not that I can think of. I'll pick up Nate at the airport later today, but I also have a...sort of a contingency plan. One of my friends will help me if...well...if anything happens." She didn't want to tell David exactly what she feared, but she had already planned to call Cassie and maybe Jubilee. And there was always 9-1-1.

He seemed to read her mind. "There's always 9-1-1. And of course, you can call me. But I hope it doesn't come to that."

"Thank you." She turned to leave the office. "And thank you again for the roses. They're absolutely beautiful."

"I hope you enjoy them."

Back at her desk, she took a picture of the roses and texted it to Cassie. A few seconds later, Cassie texted back, "Wow!" so Abigail knew she was awake and ready for her day. She punched Cassie's number.

Cassie answered on the second ring. "Beautiful flowers! What gives? Has Nate turned over a romantic leaf?"

"No way. They're from David...well, from the company really...to congratulate me on my good work."

"Way to go, girlfriend! You deserve them."

"Thanks, but I'm calling about something else. I'm going to need your help, probably tonight, because I'm not sure how everything is going to play out when Nate gets home."

"You've got it. And Rick, too. We'll both come. I'll bring my baseball bat."

Abigail laughed. "Oh, I can just picture how threatening you'll look. A pregnant woman swinging a bat."

"Hey! I was on the state championship softball team in high school. Third base. I can still swing at a wicked pitch even if I *am* thirty pounds heavier and carrying the next generation."

"Right. Well, bring your bat if you must and yes, probably Rick as well."

Abigail shifted uncomfortably. "I'm going to convince Nate to go out to eat. He's always starving when he gets off the plane and sometimes he wants an enormous meal at home. But this time, we'll go somewhere. I figure that will put us in the public if he throws a fit."

"So you're going to tell him?"

"Yes. I've thought about it and I didn't sleep all night. I won't tell him everything David knows, because he and Ralph worked all day yesterday. I don't know what else they found. But Nate *is* my husband. I think I owe him an explanation, a bit of a warning."

"You don't owe this guy anything, but he is *your* hubby."

"I want him to let me go back to school. If I make him too mad, my dream of becoming a teacher won't happen. Besides, I'll need his money to enroll and pay for my tuition. I don't have that kind of cash and only Nate can give it to me. I know Jubilee wouldn't want me to manipulate my husband. She would want me to tell him the truth."

Cassie sighed. "Okay, but I think you should tread carefully here."

"I will, and if he's in a bad mood or if anything backfires, I won't tell him anything. I've lived with him for nine years. I think my intuition is pretty good. And he's never really hurt me, physically, that is. Well...not much."

Cassie warned Abigail again about being cautious, taking care of herself, setting her personal boundaries. Finally, she ran out of directives and asked, "So what's the contingency plan? When do Rick and I storm in and rescue you?"

Abigail giggled. "You make it sound like an old Western movie or something."

"Well, howdy, ma'am. How kin we hepya'?"

"Oh, stop it, silly. It's simple. If I get into any trouble or if he threatens me, I'll send you a text. Something like...I don't know...."

"How about 'Send in the cavalry'?"

"Too long. How about just 'Help'? No. Still too long. I may not have time for four letters."

"Abigail, this sounds really dangerous. Shouldn't you just call 9-1-1?"

"I may have to...later.... How about if I text you an 'H'? That stands for 'Help.' Got it?"

"Got it. But promise me, if he hits you before we can get there...."

"I know. I promise. I'll call the police."

"Okay, friend. See you later."

"Thanks, Cassie."

"You bet."

The rest of the day seemed to crawl by. Abigail kept busy but worried about what to tell Nate. Occasionally, she leaned over to smell the roses. She would have to hide them before he came back to the office. He would demand an explanation.

A little after one o-clock, a text from Nate. "Finished here. Headed for the airport. Pick me up at 5:45. Make a reservation for The Melting Pot."

She texted back. "Good idea. Will do." He was going to make this easier than she thought.

She quickly texted Cassie. "We'll be at The Melting Pot on the Plaza, sometime around six. Maybe you and Rick can park out front, in case I need to jump in your car."

"Copy that," Cassie texted back. "I'll bring my bat."

※※※

When Nate kissed her hello, Abigail smelled the alcohol. He must have had several drinks in First Class. She held his arm, pretending to lean into him, but tried to support him and keep him from weaving.

"I'll drive," he said, when they neared her Acura.

"No, you won't. You've had too much to drink."

He shrugged. Thankfully, she didn't have to argue with him in front of all the other passengers hurrying to their cars.

After they both clicked into their seat belts, she quickly maneuvered out of KCI and onto the highway. Maybe after a good dinner, she would let him sleep off his drunken stupor before she told him anything. Let him face David with a hangover.

She pulled into one of the parking garages near the restaurant and turned once again to ask, "Are you sure you want to eat here? Maybe go home and rest?"

He was already fumbling with his seat belt and shot her a dirty look. "Shut up. Let's get inside."

She tried to hold his arm when he came around to her side of the car, but he pushed her away. He plowed across the street while she followed. A car swerved and honked.

"Idiot!" Nate shouted and gave the middle finger salute.

Four parking spaces away from the entrance, Abigail recognized Cassie's car. Rick's face was hidden under his Royals baseball cap. Cassie sat in the front seat and sure enough, she waved a baseball bat.

Abigail followed Nate into the restaurant and gave their name to the hostess who showed them to their table. Nate stumbled a bit, then plopped into a chair. "Bring me a bottle of Merlot," he said.

"Coffee," said Abigail. "Black and strong." She probably wouldn't sleep tonight anyway. Might as well have some caffeine available and try to convince Nate to drink some.

She excused herself. "I'll be in the ladies room for a minute."

"Couldn't you do that before you left the office?" Nate growled. "Oh, all right. Hurry up."

Thankfully, no other women occupied any of the stalls. She pulled her cell phone out of her purse and called Cassie. "He's too drunk to pay attention to anything I say tonight. I'm not going to tell him anything. You and Rick go on home. I'll talk to you later."

"Are you sure? If he's drunk, he might cause a problem. Don't you want to stay at our house tonight? I already put clean sheets on the guest bed."

"No, but thanks. I'll be fine. I'll placate him tonight as much as possible, then wait 'till morning to decide what to do."

"Okay, but we're only a few miles away. Text me an 'H' and we'll come running."

"Right. Thanks."

She stayed a little longer in the ladies room, then returned to the table. Nate had obviously ordered for both of them. He dipped a carrot into the cheese fondue, then followed it with a piece of sourdough bread. A plate of shrimp sat near his elbow. Abigail moved it toward the middle of the table.

"Why'd you do that?"

"Just avoiding any accidents." She started on her salad, dipping a piece of rye bread into the same cheese fondue. "How did it go in Illinois?"

He frowned. "The director is a jerk. He isn't filling the rooms with new residents when somebody croaks. Probably have to replace him."

"That's too bad. Couldn't you talk to him and give him another chance?"

"Of course I talked to him. What do ya' think I've been doing this week? What a stupid suggestion!"

"I was just asking a question. No need to bite my head off in a restaurant in front of everybody."

"Don't tell me what to do. Just eat and shut up. I've been dealing with idiots all week. I don't need another stupid remark from you."

Stupid? She was smart enough to figure out his little secret, but this definitely wasn't the time or the place to let him know what she had done. He drank a bit of her coffee, then followed it with another glass of Merlot. She concentrated on her salad.

His cell phone buzzed. He took it out of his pocket and fumbled with it. "Hmm. A text from Dave. A meeting in his office with Ralph, tomorrow morning at nine. Wonder what's up. Probably wants to know the details about Illinois…or maybe something with the Pennsylvania contract." He stared at Abigail. "Did you hear anything? Did Dave say anything about the new site?"

"No. Nothing about Pennsylvania." *But we did talk about you and how you've been cheating the residents.* Best to wait until morning. He would be sober and able to understand what she was talking about. Or maybe let David handle it.

She focused on cutting a piece of cucumber into smaller pieces and tried not to think about tomorrow. Nate wolfed down his shrimp entrée and emptied the last of the Merlot bottle into his glass. "You about done?" he mumbled, then belched into his napkin.

"Yes. Let's go home."

He managed to pull his credit card out of his wallet and scribbled his name across the bottom of the receipt. When he stood, it took him a moment to get his bearings. He accepted her hand on his arm as she steered him out of the restaurant and toward the parking garage.

As soon as he buckled his seat belt, he leaned back and closed his eyes. He began to snore before they turned onto I-35 and headed for home. Abigail sighed. She turned off the radio and drove in the silence of the night, wondering how Nate was going to take the news when he met with David.

Maybe Cassie was right. Don't tell him anything. Drive to work in the morning and pretend nothing was wrong. Let Nate face the consequences.

On the other hand, she wanted him to know how much of an impact his actions made on others. She wanted him to realize she had been the one to convince David not to terminate his position. Perhaps Nate would finally understand she was smart enough to go back to school and earn her degree.

She steered into the garage and nudged him, but he was completely out. With his dead weight, she could not possibly lift him out of the car. Let him sleep it off for a few hours, then help him into the house and into bed. At least she wouldn't have to tell him anything tonight. She could enjoy a few hours of peace before Nate's world and maybe hers exploded.

CHAPTER TWENTY-EIGHT

She wasn't sure when she fell asleep or when Nate came to bed. But at some point, she felt him move beside her and throw his arm around her. The alarm soon buzzed. She slipped out from under the sheets and hurried into the bathroom. Nate groaned.

She looked at herself in the mirror. Her eyes seemed too bright. Too many restless nights. Maybe when this mess was over, she would take advantage of Cassie's hospitality and schedule a retreat at her house, sleep in the luxurious guest room and forget about everything for a couple of days.

She brushed through her hair, smiling at the thought of the auburn wig she hid under the sofa cushion. She remembered how David had stared at her, obviously impressed with the blue dress and the change in her hair. Forget that for now. Today was a new day and an important one.

She passed Nate in the hallway as he slumped toward the shower. "I'll get some coffee started," she said.

He mumbled something and soon, she heard the water running. She finished dressing and hurried downstairs. The homey smell of dark roast filled the kitchen as she scrambled a few eggs and added some bacon bits. She scraped butter across the toast and fixed Nate's plate first, then her own. After she carried both plates to the table, she sipped some tea and waited.

It wasn't long before he came into the kitchen, his hair still wet, the stray wave falling across his forehead. He seemed confident and whistled a tune. Obviously, the night of sleep and the morning shower had refreshed him although shadows lingered under his eyes.

For a moment, she felt sorry for this man with whom she had shared nine years. Maybe he could still change. Maybe they could find a way to have a decent marriage, although she felt no passion for him, no confidence in the possibility of happiness. She only felt a sense of duty.

Make it through this day. Do what was right. Help him understand why she had felt it was important to be honest about the residents' activities. She was tired of lying, sick of the secrets and the way her life had turned into one problem after another. They had spent nine years together. Surely she owed him the truth.

She tried to eat a few bites, but her stomach felt sour. She tried another sip of tea. Finally, she carried her plate to the sink and washed her breakfast down the garbage disposal. When she turned around, he was checking his phone for messages.

"Nate, I need to tell you something."

"Hmm?" He poked at his phone.

She moved closer. "I think it's time you knew the truth. Please, listen to me."

He groaned and set down his phone. "All right. What?"

"I haven't been happy for a long time. You know I've wanted to go back to school, and I think you've been unfair to me...about so many things. The way you've treated me, ignoring my needs, your words like when you call me stupid...."

His jaw clenched. His pointer finger tapped the table. He picked up his phone. "Is this one of your cycle days? I don't know what you're talking about."

"I'm talking about my life...our life together...and what a mess it is. I'm trying to be honest with you. Cassie and I didn't go to a Bible study. We went to a Life Limits Class where I learned about self-respect and authenticity, how to stand up for myself and speak my truth."

She took a deep breath, forced herself not to cry. "You've sucked the life out of me, and you don't even care. I've felt as lifeless as the beige pantsuits you've made me wear. I'm so used to being your victim, your soul-sucking has been my comfort zone. Well, not anymore, Nate. Something has to change."

He stood up and moved closer. "So...you were lying about a Bible study? Do you know how perverted that is? What else have you been lying about? What have you done?"

She patted the pocket of her blazer to make certain her cell phone was ready. "Your meeting with David this morning. I know what it's about."

She reached on the granite-topped island for a recipe card and a black Sharpie. She wrote LSPB0826 on the card and handed it to Nate. He looked at it, then glared at her.

She cleared her throat. "I know what this means, and I know what you've been doing. You remember my friend, Ruth? David's great grandmother? She told me how some of her friends were being charged for extra activities. She asked me to find out about it and I promised her I would. I figured out your code, the way you reverse letters, and I called Ralph...."

"You did what?" His fist slammed the table. A vein in his neck pulsed.

She took out her cell phone and texted "H" to Cassie. Then she faced him. Oddly enough, she felt no fear. Only a numb certainty that she had done the right thing. "Yes. I called Ralph. We figured out how you hid the extra charges. I took the evidence and showed it to David."

She watched the changes of emotion on his face. Shock turned to intense anger, then his eyes hardened. Like an evil mask, he turned red, then rage-filled purple. He threw his coffee cup against the back door. It hit the baseboard and chunked off a piece of wood that flew up and landed on the window sill. He picked up his plate and threw it toward her. She ducked behind the kitchen island as the plate flew over her and hit the refrigerator. Ice fell out of the ice maker.

"You bitch! How dare you! You're gonna' pay for this."

She ran toward the front door, but he was faster and so much bigger. He grabbed her blazer and yanked her back. She screamed as her cell phone fell out of her hand. It slid across the wood floor. His hands around her neck, tightened against her windpipe.

A cloudy memory from Life Limits class. Jubilee. She clasped her hands together under his chin and thrust them upward with all her might. His head snapped back, and his eyes closed. His grip loosened.

She coughed, then plunged toward her cell phone, fell to the floor and punched 9-1-1. She tried to scramble to her feet, but Nate grabbed her ankle and pulled her toward him. He twisted the phone out of her hand. She kicked at his chest and reached for the umbrella stand.

She swung the umbrella toward him. The tip sliced into his cheek. He shook his head and blood zigzagged across his face. The side of his mouth drooped into a cockeyed position. With a grasp toward her, he fell.

Panting, she reached for her phone. A female voice asked, "What is your emergency?"

She managed to croak out the address. "Send an ambulance. And the police. I think I just killed my husband."

Seconds later, the front window crashed. Rick fell onto the living room floor, Cassie's bat in his hand. The security system kicked in and wailed its warning. Lights flashed throughout the foyer.

Someone pounded on the front door. Cassie's soprano pitch even higher than usual. "Open up in there! Rick! Abigail! Let me in!"

"You all right?" Rick asked Abigail on his way to the front door.

She nodded. A siren wailed in the distance, then grew louder. Cassie waddled through the front door, knelt beside Abigail and folded her in her arms. Rick bent over Nate and felt for a pulse.

Abigail sobbed and coughed. "He tried to choke me. I remembered what Jubilee taught us. It worked. Then I reached for the umbrella, and his face did this weird thing. I don't know what happened. Is he dead?"

"No," said Rick. Then he moved aside as three paramedics and two police officers stormed through the front door.

CHAPTER TWENTY-NINE

After the doctor checked Abigail's vitals, he lifted her chin and stared at her for several seconds. "You are one lucky woman. A few more minutes and your windpipe would have been crushed. It's a good thing you called 9-1-1. I can't tell you how many women I patch up in the ER—women who become victims, women who should have called for help months, even years ago. Good for you."

"Any word on my husband? I hit him with the umbrella."

"The neurologist is finishing scans. He'll have some news for you in a little while." The doctor shook his head. "You hit him with an umbrella?"

"I cut his cheek. It was bleeding."

The doctor touched her shoulder. "An umbrella could never do the damage we saw in your husband's initial exam. This is much more serious than a facial injury."

She cleared her throat. "More serious? What do you mean?"

"We'll let you know when we finish further tests. You take care of yourself now. And don't be surprised if your voice sounds a little hoarse, feels a bit raw. You might want to drink something soothing, like hot tea with honey." He wrote on her chart, then left the room.

A nurse helped her off the table, then pointed toward the waiting room. "Your friends are in there, ma'am. Have a seat in this wheelchair and I'll take you to them."

"Oh, I don't need a wheelchair."

"It's policy, ma'am, and you've been through a shock. You may not be as steady as you think."

In the far corner of the waiting room, Rick flipped through a Sports Illustrated magazine. Cassie held a bag of Cheetos and munched on a handful. Even from the doorway, Abigail saw the orange rim around her mouth. Next to her sat David, who sipped out of a Styrofoam cup. He stared upward at the TV which was tuned to CNN. Something about a plane crash in Indonesia.

Cassie saw Abigail first. She dropped the bag of Cheetos and hurried across the room. "Are you all right? The doctor told us you had a close call. Oh, girlfriend! You almost got killed." She grabbed Abigail's head and pressed it into her chest.

Abigail felt the beat of Cassie's heart. The baby kicked. She patted Cassie on the back, then coughed and muttered, "Can't breathe. Let me go."

"Oh, sorry. But are you okay?"

"Yes. The doctor said I was lucky."

Rick and David stood. "More than lucky," David said. "Your friends filled me in on what happened. I'd say you were mighty brave."

Abigail shook her head, trying to clear some of the fuzziness. "But…how did you find out…to come here…to the hospital? Nate was supposed to meet with you today. Wasn't it today?"

Cassie put her arm around Abigail and helped her out of the wheelchair. "I called David. When he got here, Rick told him everything that happened. How we got your 'H' text, how we drove like idiots to your house, how my man came stormin' through the window. Wasn't he just somethin' else?"

Rick shrugged, but grinned at Cassie.

David came forward and touched Abigail's arm. "They told me Nate had you by the throat. My God, Abigail! I'm so sorry! If I had been there, I would have killed him."

She felt a little woozy. "I need to sit down."

David led her to one of the chairs, then settled beside her. Cassie and Rick sat across from them. Cassie held out her bag of Cheetos. "Want some?" she asked.

"No, thanks, but a drink of water would be nice. My throat is sore."

David jumped up and rushed toward the nurse's station where he asked for a bottle of water. The nurse pointed him toward the water fountain in the hallway. In a few minutes, he returned, carrying a paper cup with water sloshing out the side.

"Whoa there, fella'," Rick said. "Slow down or there won't be anything left to drink."

The four of them sat in silence as the CNN anchor continued to broadcast the latest news. Medical personnel passed the waiting room, their colorful scrubs a pastel blend with the mauve-painted walls around them. Other families huddled together in various parts of the room.

Cassie finished the bag of Cheetos and crumpled it up, then tossed it to Rick. "Could you get me a Coke, babe?"

Rick stood up and almost collided with a doctor who marched into the waiting room. His stethoscope swinging, his hand clutched a clipboard. "Mrs. Calebian?"

Abigail stood, her head clear although her heart dreaded what the doctor might say. "Yes," she said. "I'm here." She could feel David's hand touching hers.

"Ma'am, your husband has suffered a hemorrhagic stroke, a bleeding in the brain. At this point, we don't know if it's a complete rupture or if it's merely a bleed. He may also have an aneurism, a weakness in the vessel wall. His blood pressure is high, but we feel we need to get in there and find the extent of the damage, try to clip off the bleeding and control the impairment. We'll need your permission for surgery."

"Of course. Whatever you need to do."

"A stroke," said David. "Is he paralyzed?"

The doctor nodded. "At this point, there is some paralysis of his right side, but again—we don't know the extent of the damage nor do we know if it will be temporary or permanent. Since he's fairly young...." He glanced at the chart. "Yes. Early thirties. He has a good chance for survival. We anticipate several hours in surgery and then recovery. We'll keep you posted. If you leave the hospital, give the nurses your cell phone so we can contact you."

"Thank you," Abigail said.

"Yes. Thank you," echoed David. He sat down heavily. "A stroke. Wow! That's really serious."

Abigail looked at Cassie and Rick. "You go home. There's no reason for all of us to be here. We can't do anything except wait."

"I'm not leaving," said David.

Rick put his arm around Cassie. "I'm taking Cassie home whether she wants to go or not. I think she needs to rest and besides, we have more Cheetos in our pantry."

"Funny guy," said Cassie. She kissed Abigail on the cheek. "We'll come back in a few hours. Can I bring you anything?"

"No, I don't think so. Wait. Yes. Bring my wig and my purple scarf from Life Limits Class. They're under the middle sofa cushion."

Cassie smiled. "You got it."

After Cassie and Rick left, Abigail walked over to the window. She watched them cross the parking lot and climb into their car. Rick held the door open for Cassie. "They're such wonderful people," she said as she felt David near.

"Yep."

"They saved my life."

"You saved your own life. Sure, they got there in the nick of time, but it was your courage that saved you." He slipped his arm around her. "You're smart, brave and beautiful. You're an asset to the Villas and to the executive office. No matter what happens with Nate, I hope you never leave."

She turned to face him. "But I will leave. I have to. Even if Nate survives this stroke, I'll be leaving the Villas. I want to become a teacher, and I'm determined to go back to school to make that happen. With or without my husband. In fact, you can consider today as the beginning of my two-week notice."

"If that's what you want, then go for it. I'll support you however I can."

They sat without speaking. David stood up to refill his coffee cup. "Do you want anything? Need anything?"

She answered, "No, but thank you for asking."

※※※

The clock on the wall ticked toward two o'clock when Cassie and Rick returned. Rick carried a large basket he set on the floor. He passed out bottles of water and moved the magazines off the table, then whipped open a red and white checkered tablecloth.

"Just like a picnic," he said. He reached into the basket and pulled out several varieties of sandwiches, then a jar of dill pickles, "For Cassie," he said, with a grin, "and anyone else who wants one." Then two bunches of red grapes and a bag of carrot sticks. He plopped a bag of Oreos in the middle of the table.

Cassie handed Abigail a large Macy's bag filled to the brim. Abigail rummaged in the bag, recognizing her silk pajamas and matching robe, slippers, her cosmetic bag filled with several items, another bag with toothbrush, floss and toothpaste, a pair of sweats, clean underwear, the wig and the beautiful purple scarf. At the bottom of the bag was a large package of Ghirardelli chocolates.

"You thought of everything." She kissed Cassie's cheek.

"Sorry it took us a while. We went back over to your house and while I grabbed the things I thought you'd need, Rick boarded up the broken window. We talked to the police. They said they'll patrol past the house several times tonight to make sure everything is okay. Rick called the security company and they reset the system. Even if you don't go home tonight, everything will be safe."

"You guys are the best."

"Yeah. We know. Let's eat!"

Abigail wondered how they could have such a good time, eating together and telling corny jokes when just a few doors away, Nate's life lay in the hands of the surgeon. She noticed tiny worry lines on David's forehead. He often looked at the clock as if he wondered how long it took to cut into someone's brain and fish around for a remedy.

She wolfed down a pimiento cheese sandwich, surprised by how delicious it tasted. Only seven hours since she had fixed breakfast and forced herself to eat a few bites. So much had happened since then.

Rick opened the Oreos and tossed a couple at David. "Are you an eat-the-whole-thing type of guy or a take-it-apart guy?"

David chomped on both Oreos at once. Then he swallowed some water. "Does that answer your question?"

Abigail twirled open her Oreo and started to lick the white center when the neurologist entered the waiting room, a white cap perched on his head. Cassie stood and offered him a handful of grapes.

"No, thank you," he said with a tired smile. He took Abigail's hand and said, "It's not as bad as we originally thought. The right side of your husband's brain is affected. We anticipate some paralysis, so he'll need rehab and physical therapy. This was a major event, and we've done everything possible at this point. He's in recovery now. Then we'll move him to a private room. You can stay there with him, if you'd like."

Abigail felt numb. "Thank you for all you've done."

When the doctor left, Cassie hugged her. "Oh, girlfriend, this is awful. What can we do?"

"Nothing, I guess. You guys go on home and David, you need to get back to work. I'll be all right. I think I'll take a nap."

David nodded. "I'll check in at the office, call Samuel and the rest of the board members, make sure everything is okay at the Villas. I'll come back tonight. Would you like me to bring supper?"

"I guess. I don't know."

"Well, I'm not leaving," Cassie said as she sat back down and reached for the Oreos. "I'll stay until David gets back. But I know Rick needs to get to work."

"Yep," said Rick. "Want me to take the picnic basket and the leftover food back with me?"

"Touch that food and you die," said Cassie. "I'll bring home any leftovers."

Rick kissed her. "Yeah, right. We haven't had leftovers since you got pregnant." He patted Abigail's arm. "Take care. I'll be back later."

"Thanks, Rick. Thanks, David. I'll be okay."

"Darn right," said Cassie. "'Cause I'm here." She reached for another Oreo.

CHAPTER THIRTY

The next few days blurred together as Abigail lived in Nate's hospital room. Cassie, Rick and David took turns sitting with her, brought snacks and walked with her up and down the hallways. Nate remained hooked to machines, but some of his vitals began to improve. Occasionally, Pastor Dennis or an elder from church visited and prayed over Nate, held Abigail's hand and assured her God could heal her husband. She listened respectfully but seldom replied.

On the fifth day, Nate began to wake up. He groaned and struggled to open his eyes. Abigail hurried to the nurse's station and soon the room was filled with medical personnel. All of Nate's vitals were checked and recorded several times.

The neurologist asked, "Can you hear me, Mister Calebian? If so, blink once."

Nate blinked, and one of the nurses squeezed Abigail's hand.

"Excellent," said the doctor. "Cognitive recognition. And what about speaking? Can you tell us your first name?"

Nate struggled, his mouth working. Then he cleared his throat and whispered, "Na-a-ate."

After several more specialists confirmed the positive prognosis, Abigail suddenly found herself alone in the room. Except for the beep of the monitors, everything was quiet.

She stared at Nate, so different now from the handsome man she had married. His head had been shaved for the surgery. No more thick brown hair with a curl falling forward. The oxygen tube was in place and his cheekbones were sunken. The right side of his face drooped downward. His right arm lay useless at his side. But his eyes held anger as he followed her every movement.

He could no longer hurt her physically, verbally or emotionally. She was surprised that she felt no sorrow. She could lose nothing by being honest with him. It was time to speak her truth.

She twirled the wedding band on her finger as she moved closer to his bed. "I'm glad you woke up, Nate. A stroke is a terrible thing, and I imagine you feel quite powerless. I know that feeling."

She shuddered as she looked at the slice on his cheek. It was beginning to scab over. She needed the same healing for her soul, to scab over and let the scars mend.

"You don't have to worry about your job. When I told David how you doctored the accounts, I begged him not to fire you. You're good at development. You've always been good at everything, except to love your wife."

Her throat closed with angry tears. She coughed, then walked into Nate's bathroom and gulped some water. She took a deep breath and returned to the side of his bed. "Jubilee once told me as long as my voice is silent, I will remain invisible. And I *was* silent. I thought if I loved you enough, pleased you enough, even prayed enough—you would eventually change. I didn't recognize it, couldn't even name it as abuse for a long time. I was taught by you and by the church that I had to submit, had to obey you as the authority figure in my life.

"But they were wrong, Nate. So wrong. No one should be silent about abuse. No one has to live with evil. Not even God demands that."

He tried to say something, but his mouth and tongue struggled to work properly. She reached for the cup of water on his bedside tray and held it as he sipped from the straw. His face red from the exertion, his head fell back on the pillow.

"This is the last time I'll do anything for you, Nate. I don't mean to be unkind. I don't want to be as cruel as you were to me, but this is the end. Sometimes I can still feel your hands around my throat."

She shivered as she placed his cup back on the bedside tray. "I was afraid of you, but I was more afraid of the unknown, of what I would do without you, of who I could become. Afraid to be without the security of your money. Afraid because I didn't know how my life might change. Now I know I can trust myself to make right decisions and go forward in life, for my own sake. I'm smart enough to find another job and go back to school.

"The doctors say you'll make it through this. I know you'll be determined and work hard to get your health back. In fact, the hospital says a home health nurse can help you. I've already completed the paperwork to set that in motion.

"But I won't be there to support you. I won't give you another chance to hurt me. I'm moving forward with my life. I've already given my notice to David. I'm leaving the Villas and I'm leaving you."

As she voiced her determination, she knew her decision was final. She would carry out her life's plan, no matter what it cost her. This important step had been buried inside her, in that inner place as secretive as the tiny slip of peacock blue fabric pinned to her bra.

Her voice seemed louder, the strength of her decision resounding through her soul and into the room. "I'll start over, just like that kids' toy I told you about. I'm turning it over so the pegs are straight and tall, and I'll never allow you or anyone else to pound me down again."

She crossed the room and sat in the love seat, moved aside the blanket that covered her at night. "I suppose this is rather ugly of me, to talk like this when you can't fight back. But I don't feel any regret. You hurt me when *I* couldn't fight back, when I wasn't strong enough to know how. But never again." A peace she hadn't felt for months pulsed through her soul.

A police officer entered the room. "Ma'am," he said, holding his hat in his hand. "The nurses told me to come on in. I'm glad to see you're all right. I was one of the officers who responded to your 9-1-1 call."

"Oh, thank you," she said as she walked toward him and shook his hand. "I'm sorry I don't remember you. Everything about that day is a bit fuzzy."

"Of course. I'm here to finish my report and to ask if you're going to press charges." He looked toward Nate.

She hesitated for a moment, then knew what to say. "As you can see, Officer, my husband is already in a type of jail. He's had a stroke and according to the doctors, he'll need months of rehab. I don't think arresting him would even be feasible. However, I will be filing a restraining order so he can never come near me again."

"Yes, ma'am. That sounds like a good plan." He pulled out one of his business cards and handed it to her. "If you need anything, you can call me."

The officer left, and Abigail moved toward Nate. "Did you understand what I just said? I'll not be pressing charges against you, but you will do something important for me. You will give me my freedom. Do you understand?"

She watched as his face began to redden, then gradually paled. With a glare, he managed to croak out one sentence, "I…hate…you."

She gasped and stepped back, surprised at the venom in his voice. Throughout all the bruisings and verbal cruelty, even with all the raping—she had never imagined Nate hated her. But his words confirmed her decision. She was grateful for each step forward that led to this day.

She swallowed the hurt, the finality of a marriage ended. Her voice raw, she spoke her final declaration. "I'm sorry you feel that way, Nate, although I guess I shouldn't be surprised. I don't hate you, but I pity you. Your choices have led to this moment. I'll be hiring a lawyer. She will contact you."

Abigail gathered her things and glanced once more at her husband. She took a deep breath as she left his room, walked down the hallway and punched the elevator button for the first floor. She squinted against the sunshine and filled her lungs with the late July air. She was grateful Cassie and Rick had driven her car to the hospital's parking lot, just in case she needed it. After she turned the key in the ignition, she called Cassie.

"I need to do something for myself. Can I borrow some money to get a new hairdo? Want to come with?"

"Absolutely."

※※※

At the salon, Abigail told George, "Time to strip off this dye. Make me look like myself again, with highlights." Cassie watched and listened as Abigail related her conversation with Nate.

"You told him you wanted your freedom?"

"Sure did. It felt great, but also kind of sad. It's weird."

George laid down his scissors, grabbed his silk handkerchief and blew his nose.

After Abigail drove Cassie home, she stopped at the grocery store to pick up the ingredients for her brownies and a few items for herself. A plate full of brownies would be her thank-you to the medical staff. It would feel good to be alone in her kitchen, to smell up the house with chocolate and do whatever she wanted without Nate's interference.

When she pulled up to the house and punched the garage door opener, she was surprised to see the front window had been replaced. Good old Rick and Cassie. They must have fixed it themselves or called the insurance company to set everything in motion.

She put all the groceries away and kicked off her shoes. She would put them away later. No, she didn't have to put them away. Nate wouldn't be coming home to make sure everything was in its proper place. She could mess up the house any way she wanted.

For now, she needed a shower and a clean change of clothes. She stood in the closet for a minute, then ran to the garage for a large box. She wanted every reminder of her past life gone, to move forward with nothing hanging over her, nothing dragging her down.

Surprised by how energized she felt, she carried the box upstairs and started filling it with all the beige and black clothes. Black pants, beige knit tops, taupe blazers. She smiled as she envisioned carrying the box into a nonprofit that provided career clothes for women.

Finished. The empty hangers, a visual of Nate's control, now hung askew in haphazard bundles. All that remained were a couple pairs of sweats and the beautiful blue dress. Abigail added another item to her mental list: *As soon as I find another job, go shopping for colorful clothes.*

She pulled off her wedding ring and considered the Tiffany diamonds, then emptied her jewelry armoire into a plastic bag. All the gifts Nate had given her through the years. They were hers and worth thousands. She would use them to secure her future.

She picked up her wedding band and rubbed it into between her fingers. "I don't owe you an explanation, Nate. I don't owe you anything. In fact, *you* are the one who owes me for a lifetime of pain." She threw her wedding band into the bag.

She fluffed her new hairdo and looked at herself in the mirror. Her auburn bob, identical to the wig, looked even better because it was real, her true self. She unwound the purple scarf from around her neck and picked out another pair of sweats. After she showered and dressed, she pinned the peacock blue fabric piece on the outside of her T-shirt and smiled at her reflection in the mirror.

"Hello, Abigail. Source of joy." Then she hurried downstairs to stir up the brownies.

The smell of chocolate filled the house as Abigail went downstairs to the office. She clicked on the computer to search for online catalogs of universities and their local satellites. After printing off pages of information, she compared tuition rates at the various colleges in the area. More than anything right now, she wanted to be around people who shared her hope for the future.

Some of that hope began to seep into her soul. Even though the future seemed uncertain, at least she felt more empowered. She had stated what she wanted and now she would reach for what she needed.

She scooped the brownies onto a flowery paper plate, then stretched Saran Wrap around them. Tomorrow she would take them to the nurses' station. She rummaged in the kitchen for a note card. "I appreciate all you've done to help my husband."

She walked into the living room. *My husband.* It should have represented a sweet sentiment, a safe person with whom to share life. But it didn't turn out that way. A pang of regret filtered through her soul. She wished things could have ended differently, wanted so much more for her marriage, for their life together.

No use living in the regret of what could have been. She sighed and out of habit, straightened Nate's Forbes magazine on the ottoman.

She stretched out on the sofa and covered up with a light blanket. "I'll never spend another night in the bed where Nate slept." The sofa felt comfortable and soft. In only a few seconds, she was asleep, secure in the dreamy cocoon of imagining her new life.

No Visible Scars

CHAPTER THIRTY-ONE

When Abigail met with Jubilee, she cried through the first minutes of the session. "I don't know what's wrong with me," she said. "I wasn't this upset when everything ended with Nate."

Jubilee patted her hand. "Many women who go through abuse find their emotions numbed. You're probably letting go of the stored-up grief, plus you've been through several transitions. We need to release emotional pressure, and tears are one of the gifts God gives us for that release."

She blew her nose. "Well, I've certainly had enough release today. I'm exhausted."

"You may feel extra tired for a while. Healthy grieving takes a lot of energy, but in the end you'll feel much better."

"I think I need to grieve through my entire lifetime, starting with the loss of Mama, my shattered dreams, the sham of my marriage with Nate…everything. And I know I'm supposed to forgive. I'm not sure what that looks like."

"Forgiveness is a process. You may need to give it more time and forgive in pieces. But I'm here to help you. Let's take it one step at a time."

"I like that idea. One step at a time toward becoming my true self." She wound the purple and gold scarf around her neck, then reached into her tangerine-colored bag. "You want to see a picture of Cassie's baby?"

Jubilee reached eagerly for Abigail's cell phone and gazed at the picture. "Oh my goodness! Look at that precious child. All those golden curls, just like Cassie."

Abigail giggled. "I got to hold her right after she was born, and I could swear she smiled at me. She has Rick's eyes and sometimes, the most sober look on her face. They named her Kendsey Joy. Cassie says partly for me. They want her to grow up to be a strong woman."

"And you *are* strong. Strong and beautiful, source of joy. Someday your tears will become more hope-filled. It *will* get better, Abigail. You'll move beyond the victim mentality, past trying to merely survive and then you'll really soar. Maybe you'll even love again."

"I'm not sure about that. Right now, it's hard to trust any man. First, I want to finish school, secure a teaching position and prove I can live alone." She put her phone back in her bag and stroked the nubby texture. "Oh, I didn't tell you. David, the CEO, gave me a great severance package and my lawyer helped me fight for a good settlement from Nate. So I bought a condo near campus, and I'm working part-time at the student union."

"Good for you. Keep setting those personal boundaries."

"I will, but I sort of feel guilty about one thing. I can't seem to make myself go back to church. I tried for a few weeks, but I didn't fit in. I'm not a couple now, not part of the traditional family model. The singles group seems to focus on finding a mate, and I'm not interested. Every

Sunday, they pray for Nate's recovery, but I don't know if anyone prays for me." She reached for another Kleenex.

Jubilee nodded. "God knows what you've been through and although it's important to have the support of others, it's okay to take a sabbatical from church. In fact, several of my clients live stream their church services from home."

"That's a great idea. I'll try that."

"Give yourself time, Abigail. Time to heal. Eventually, you can visit other churches and find one that fits. Or find a small group of people who will support you outside the church building. God is with you whether you're sitting in a pew, drinking coffee with Cassie or taking a bubble bath. He's everywhere and always loving you. Let him gently love you back to wholeness."

She took a deep breath and felt as if something had opened in her heart, the shame leaking out while joy took its place. "Let God gently love me. Yes. I'll do that. Thanks. See you next week?"

"Same time. Same place," said Jubilee as she opened the door.

"Oh, I almost forgot. I wanted to tell you about my cat. Nate would never let us have pets, so I drove to Wayside Waifs and rescued an older cat. She's kind of a tabby, sort of orange and white with a brown spot on one paw. She sleeps with me and cuddles close."

"And what did you name her?"

"I call her Libby. Short for Liberty. Appropriate, right?"

No Visible Scars

※ ※ ※

Throughout the next months, Abigail focused on enjoying her life and the gradual path to emotional healing. She helped Cassie set up Smart Art, attended classes and kept her grade average at 4.0. She baby-sat Kendsey Joy, bounced her on her lap and read "The Cat in the Hat" over and over.

One weekend, she and Cassie strolled with the baby through Art in the Park. Abigail found a sparkly turquoise frame. She placed the scrap of peacock blue inside. *A reminder of what you taught me, Ruth. To live with beauty and joy and never hide my true self again.*

Sometimes, sadness overwhelmed her as she regretted the years with Nate. Other times, she recoiled with anger at the way he treated her. She screamed out her anger with herself, for not setting boundaries earlier, for letting him take advantage of her and control her. But as Jubilee reminded her, she had done the best she could at the time. Living in past regrets would keep her from joy.

Most days, she felt relief that her current life was headed in a more positive direction. Her invisible scars took longer to heal than she expected, but with Jubilee's help and the support of Cassie and Rick, she felt herself growing stronger each month.

※ ※ ※

A year after the divorce was final, Abigail mixed a batch of brownies for the staff at the student union. She was grateful she had work to do and friendly people in her life.

The warm aroma of cocoa spread to the bedroom as she showered, brushed through her hair and found a pair of sparkly gold earrings. Then she pulled on her favorite jeans, a sleeveless yellow tunic and bronze sandals that showcased her turquoise pedicure.

The oven timer dinged. She stuck a toothpick in the brownies, then set the pan on the counter to cool.

The doorbell rang. Startled out of her fifth nap of the day, Libby jumped up from the window seat and scampered into the bedroom.

Abigail laughed. "It's just the doorbell, silly cat. No worries." She peered through the peephole in the front door, but all she could see were red roses. Puzzled, she looked out the front drapes and saw a Jeep Wrangler parked in front of her condo.

She opened the door to David who grinned from the other side of the petals. "Thought you might need some cheering up today," he said.

"Isn't that nice? Come on in. Thanks for the flowers." She filled a yellow ceramic vase with water and arranged the bouquet.

He sniffed. "Is that brownies I smell?"

"You're just in time. A fresh batch out of the oven. How many would you like?"

"All of them," he said. "But first, I need to do something I've been thinking about for a long time. I wanted to give you space…and time." He drew closer, then hesitated. "Is it okay…if I ask you out?"

She thought for a moment. "Maybe a coffee sometime. Let's take it slow. I'll call you. Okay?" She held out her hand to seal the deal.

He gently took her hand and kissed her crooked pinky finger.

Within that safe gesture, Abigail felt another sliver of the past break away and the ripples of hope expand.

SYMPTOMS OF DOMESTIC ABUSE

Controlling behaviors	Guilty Gift-Giving
Threats	Demanding Submissiveness
Ridicule	Humiliating Remarks
Accusations	Playing Mind Games
Teasing and Name-Calling	Forceful Sexual Advances
Ignoring	Rape
Hostile Anger	Jealousy
Silent Treatments	Any Physical Violence
Destroying Objects	Not Taking her Seriously
Withholding Approval	Making Her Ask for Money
Withholding Affection	Snooping in her Mail / Purse
Emotional Detachment	Constantly Checking on Her
Jokes about Her	Negative Comparisons
Threatening to Leave	Good Guy / Bad Guy
Degrading Her in Public	Stalking Her
Empty Promises	

Using the Bible or Religious Traditions to Put Down Women

ABIGAIL'S BROWNIES

2/3 cup shortening
1 ½ cups packed brown sugar
1 TB water
1 tsp vanilla extract
2 eggs
1 ½ cups all purpose flour
1/3 cup organic baking cocoa
½ tsp salt
¼ tsp baking soda
½ tsp baking powder
2 cups (12 oz) dark chocolate chips (preferably Ghirardelli)
1 can blueberry pie filling (the secret ingredient)

    In a large mixing bowl, cream shortening, sugar, water and vanilla. Beat in eggs.
    Combine flour, cocoa, salt, baking soda and baking powder. Gradually add to creamed mixture and beat just until blended.
    Stir in chocolate chips and blueberry pie filling.
    Spoon into 8x12 pan. Bake at 375 for 30 minutes. Cool and cut.

ACKNOWLEDGEMENTS

No book ever makes it to the publisher without the support of those who believe in its message. It literally takes a village. "No Visible Scars" has been in process for over 10 years. During that time, the village has multiplied.

The Saturday Sisters who constantly encourage me and let me be real. Thanks to Janet, Susan, Ginger, Sharon and Deb – who lives in heaven.

My critique group who kept me on task and sharpened the prose. Thanks to Jane, SuZan, Sara, Karen and Sally.

Thanks to the beta readers who spent their precious time reading, then wrote an endorsement and posted a review.

The brave women I met in various counseling and coaching ministries. You inspired me even as we wept together at the pain of abuse.

Thanks to my son, Caleb Thesman, for the perfect title.

Paula Koch shared in the cost of the Denver writers conference where I pitched the idea to an agent.

Dori Tompkins shared her story with vulnerability and authenticity. As an RN, she also told me some of the side effects of a hemorrhagic stroke.

Jane Tucker drove me to the airport so I could meet an agent and pitch the book.

Many thanks to my patrons who believe in my words and help support this mission.

Thanks to Molly Totoro who gave me the perfect line, "If we do not use our voices, we remain invisible."

Molly and her husband Geoff believed in the story and its significance. They shared their hotel points so I could stay at a beautiful hotel in Denver and meet with an agent.

Thanks to Karen Frommer who gave me the perfect title for Life Limits Class.

Kathy Stone shared her story and reminded me how sexual assault can happen, even within marriage.

I am grateful to Natasha Hanova of Rare Bird Editing for her insightful thoughts and her brilliance in catching the problems that might have derailed the book.

Thanks to Sarah Meiers of moshdesigns for the beautiful cover and her patience as we worked to make the design what it needed to be.

GateWay of Hope—a nonprofit organization for women in the Kansas City Metro. Through counseling, coaching and support groups, you are helping women become who God created them to be. www.gwhope.org.

Finally, I am grateful to the original Abigail whose story lives in the Old Testament book of First Samuel. Smart, beautiful and brave—she reminds us that God does not want any of his daughters to live within destructive relationships.

ABOUT THE AUTHOR

RJ Thesman is the author of ten books, a certified writing coach, a Biblical counselor and a Stephen minister. Thesman has worked in numerous nonprofit organizations and on church staff where she met women who live within destructive relationships. Their courage and the Biblical story of Abigail inspired Thesman to write "No Visible Scars."

As a Certified Writing Coach, RJ Thesman loves to help other writers birth their words. She excels at brainstorming, developing writing plans, accountability and helping her clients reach their goals. She is writing a series of coaching books for writers. "Setting and Reaching Your Writing Goals" and "5 Strategies for Social Media Engagement" were both released in 2017.

Thesman also holds a Bachelor of Science degree in Education. Besides the 10 books, her work appears in 700+ articles and in 14 anthologies.

Thesman is a member of the National Association of Professional Women, the Kansas Authors Club, the Heart of America Christian Writer's Network, the Fellowship of Christian Writers and the American Association of Christian Counselors.

She enjoys teaching workshops, speaking at various venues, reading, gardening and cooking—especially anything with blueberries.

You can follow RJ Thesman on Facebook, Twitter, LinkedIn and Goodreads. Check out her website at: https://RJThesman.net.

Also by RJ Thesman

Hope Shines

Sometimes They Forget

5 Strategies for Social Media Engagement

Setting & Reaching Your Writing Goals

19 Tips for Starting Over Single

The Unraveling of Reverend G

Intermission for Reverend G

Final Grace for Reverend G

The Plain Path

Made in the USA
Columbia, SC
06 July 2018